The Apocalypse Collection

Ancient Visions of the Afterlife, Judgment Day, and the Second Coming of Christ

A Modern Translation

Adapted for the Contemporary Reader

Various Ancient Writers

Translated by Tim Zengerink

© Copyright 2025
All rights reserved.

It is not legal to reproduce, duplicate, or transmit any part of this document in either electronic means or in printed format. Recording of this publication is strictly prohibited and any storage of this document is not allowed unless with written permission from the publisher except for the use of brief quotations in a book review.

This book contains works of fiction. Any resemblance to persons living or dead, or places, events, or locations is purely coincidental.

Table of Contents

Preface - Message to the Reader 1

Introduction 4

The Apocalypse of Abraham 10

    Introduction to the Apocalypse of Abraham 10

The Vision of Ezra 22

    Introduction 22
    Vision I 23
    Vision II 31
    Vision III 37
    Vision V 62
    Vision VI 68
    Vision VII 73

The Apocalypse of Peter 79

The Apocalypse of Paul 83

    Introduction 83
    The Acts of Paul 84

Thank You for Reading 97

Preface - Message to the Reader

What If You Could Help Rebuild the Greatest Library in Human History?

Thousands of years ago, the Library of Alexandria stood as the crown jewel of human achievement — a sanctuary where the collected wisdom of every known civilization was gathered, preserved, and shared freely.

And then, it was lost.

Through fire, conquest, and the slow erosion of time, humanity lost not just books — but ideas, dreams, discoveries, and stories that could have changed the world forever.

Today, the Library of Alexandria lives again — and you are invited to be a part of its restoration.

Our mission is simple yet profound:

To rebuild the greatest library the world has ever known, and to translate all timeless works into every language and dialect, so that no seeker of knowledge is ever left behind again.

By joining our movement to rebuild the modern Library of Alexandria, you become part of an unprecedented mission:

- **Unlimited Access to the Greatest Audiobooks & eBooks Ever Written:**
  Instantly explore thousands of legendary works—Plato, Shakespeare, Jane Austen, Leo Tolstoy, and countless more. All

instantly available to read or listen, placing a complete literary universe at your fingertips.

- **Beautiful Paperback & Deluxe Editions at Printing Cost**

    Own any title as an elegant paperback, deluxe hardcover, or stunning collectible boxset—offered to you at true printing cost, delivered straight to your door. Build your personal Library of Alexandria, crafted for beauty, built for durability, and worthy of proud display.

- **Fresh Translations for Modern Readers—in Every Language & Dialect**

    Enjoy timeless masterpieces reimagined in clear, contemporary language—no more outdated phrases or obscure references. Alongside the original versions, we're tirelessly translating these classics into every language and dialect imaginable, ensuring accessibility and understanding across cultures and generations.

- **Join a Global Renaissance of Literature & Knowledge**

    You directly support expanding our library, publishing deluxe editions at true cost, translating works into all global languages, and bringing humanity's greatest stories to people everywhere. By joining today, you're not just preserving a legacy of masterpieces; you set in motion a powerful wave of literary accessibility.

Become a Torchbearer of Knowledge.

Join us for free now at **LibraryofAlexandria.com**

Together, we will ensure that the light of human wisdom never fades again.

With gratitude and a shared love of knowledge,
The Modern Library of Alexandria Team

Visit:

www.libraryofalexandria.com

Or scan the code below:

Introduction

Lost Visions of Heaven, Hell, and the End of Time

Since the dawn of recorded history, humanity has searched for answers to the most profound questions: What happens after death? Will the world end? Is there justice beyond this life? And if so, what does that justice look like? In response, generations of prophets, mystics, and visionaries have claimed glimpses of divine revelation. Some of their writings were included in the Bible. Others, just as ancient and spiritually profound, were left out—excluded from the canon for reasons theological, political, or practical. These lost apocalyptic texts, once revered by early Christians and Jewish believers, provide vivid and often startling insights into the final judgment, the afterlife, and the coming transformation of the world.

The Apocalypse Collection: The Lost Books of Prophecy, Heaven, and the End Times brings together some of the most powerful and mysterious of these writings. Each one offers a distinct perspective, drawing from ancient traditions to describe what lies beyond the veil of human experience. These books are not simply literary curiosities or theological oddities. They are deeply moving works of spiritual imagination that shaped early conceptions of heaven, hell, divine justice, and salvation.

This collection includes The Apocalypse of Peter, The Apocalypse of Paul, The Apocalypse of Abraham, The Book of Revelation of Peter, and The Vision of Ezra. While each text stands on its own, together they offer a sweeping narrative of divine revelation: from the immediate aftermath of death to the final battle between good and evil, and from the torments of the damned to the triumph of the righteous.

Their vivid imagery, symbolic language, and emotional urgency make them among the most powerful writings in the apocalyptic tradition.

The Apocalypse of Peter:
The Torments of Hell and the Rewards of the Righteous

Among the earliest Christian apocalyptic texts, The Apocalypse of Peter offers a terrifying and unforgettable vision of hell. Written in the second century CE, it depicts Peter being guided by Jesus through the realms of the afterlife. There, he witnesses the suffering of the wicked—torments that are uniquely suited to the sins committed in life—as well as the bliss of the righteous, who dwell in peace, light, and divine communion.

What makes this text particularly significant is its influence. Before the canonical Book of Revelation became dominant, the Apocalypse of Peter was widely read in the early Church. It was even included in some early New Testament lists before ultimately being excluded. Its vivid depictions of postmortem justice deeply influenced later Christian thought, especially the medieval imagination. Many of its themes reappear in Dante's Inferno, and its stark portrayal of divine justice continues to resonate.

Yet, the text is not merely a catalogue of horrors. It offers hope and even suggests the possibility of eventual mercy for the damned— an idea that hints at a more compassionate theology. In The Apocalypse of Peter, judgment is real, but so is God's love. It reminds us that our moral choices have eternal consequences—and that repentance and compassion are always within reach.

The Apocalypse of Paul:
A Journey Through the Heavens

Building upon the tradition of Peter's vision, The Apocalypse of Paul (also known as The Vision of Paul) expands the scope of the afterlife by offering a multi-level journey through the heavens and the torments of hell. Allegedly revealed to the Apostle Paul, this text follows the soul's journey after death and presents a highly structured cosmology of reward and punishment.

The heavens are arranged in layers, each more glorious than the last. Paul encounters angels, sees the celestial thrones, and learns the fate of souls based on their earthly deeds. The wicked are tormented by demons in elaborate and gruesome punishments, while the righteous ascend toward divine glory. The journey culminates in a vision of the throne of God and the eternal joy of the saints.

Like The Apocalypse of Peter, this text had an enormous influence on later Christian eschatology. It circulated widely in the Middle Ages and was a primary source for developing ideas of purgatory and the hierarchy of the afterlife. But beyond its graphic details, The Apocalypse of Paul offers profound insights into divine justice, mercy, and the mystery of salvation. It asks us to consider the nature of our souls, the meaning of our lives, and the hope of eternal communion with God.

The Apocalypse of Abraham:
A Jewish Vision of Cosmic Judgment

Moving from the Christian tradition to Jewish apocalyptic literature, The Apocalypse of Abraham provides a unique and powerful account of divine revelation. Attributed to Abraham, the founding patriarch of Judaism, this text takes the form of a heavenly ascent. Abraham is shown the workings of the cosmos, the corruption of the world, the judgment of the wicked, and the coming of a new creation.

This book reflects the trauma of exile, the longing for justice, and the hope of redemption. Written during a time of Roman oppression and religious persecution, it seeks to reaffirm God's covenant and provide comfort to a people in crisis. Its images are rich with symbolism: angels, thrones, cosmic battles, and the struggle between good and evil on both earthly and heavenly planes.

While Christian apocalyptic texts focus on Christ and the Church, the Apocalypse of Abraham centers on Israel's fate and the broader moral order of the world. Yet its themes—righteousness, divine judgment, messianic hope—are deeply resonant with both traditions. It offers a compelling vision of what it means to live faithfully in a broken world and to await the restoration that only God can bring.

The Revelation of Peter (Book of Revelation of Peter): An Alternative Apocalypse

Distinct from The Apocalypse of Peter, this shorter Revelation of Peter—sometimes confused with the more well-known text—offers another early Christian vision of the end times. It presents a series of prophecies and visions related to the Second Coming of Christ, the destruction of the wicked, and the resurrection of the dead.

What makes this text fascinating is its apocalyptic tone coupled with pastoral urgency. It's not just about fire and judgment, but about preparing the soul, resisting deception, and holding fast to faith in times of crisis. It speaks to communities under persecution and spiritual attack, offering them assurance that God's justice will prevail.

Though overshadowed by the canonical Book of Revelation, this text deserves renewed attention for its spiritual depth and poetic power. It enriches our understanding of how early Christians grappled with eschatological hope and fear.

The Vision of Ezra: Prophetic Insight from the Scribe of Israel

Closely tied to the apocalyptic books of Esdras, The Vision of Ezra is a prophetic and visionary work that explores the trials of the end times and the triumph of the faithful. Ezra, the scribe and reformer of the Second Temple period, is shown revelations of the coming judgment, the fate of nations, and the destiny of Israel.

Ezra's visions combine lamentation and revelation. He mourns for the suffering of his people but is comforted by angelic messages of future redemption. He learns that human history is not without purpose and that God's justice will ultimately be manifest. The text includes cosmic imagery, symbolic dreams, and moral exhortation.

As with other apocalyptic literature, The Vision of Ezra is concerned with meaning-making in the face of catastrophe. It seeks to answer the question: Where is God in our suffering? And it answers by pointing to the future—a time when evil will be judged, righteousness rewarded, and creation renewed.

The Relevance of Apocalypse Today

It is tempting to relegate these texts to the realm of myth or ancient religious curiosity. But their themes are timeless. We still ask the same questions: What is the meaning of suffering? Is there justice beyond this life? Will good ultimately triumph over evil? And what role do we play in the unfolding story of the world?

The apocalypse, in its original sense, means "unveiling"—a revealing of what is hidden. These texts do not simply predict future events. They reveal deeper truths about the human condition, the nature of God, and the moral structure of the universe. They challenge us to live with integrity, to prepare our souls, and to cultivate a hope that is grounded in something greater than ourselves.

This modern translation preserves the power and poetry of the originals while making them accessible to today's readers. Archaic phrasing has been clarified, and contextual notes offer insight into symbolic imagery and theological significance. Whether you are reading for scholarship, inspiration, or spiritual growth, these texts invite reflection, reverence, and renewal.

May the visions of Peter, Paul, Abraham, Ezra, and others guide you through the mysteries of the end times—and into the eternal light of divine truth.

The Apocalypse of Abraham

Introduction to the Apocalypse of Abraham

The Apocalypse of Abraham is an ancient text that expands on Abraham's story, describing his spiritual journey and the visions he received from God. Likely written during the late Second Temple period, this text gives insight into Jewish beliefs at the time, focusing on themes like divine justice, the origins of evil, and humanity's redemption.

The story follows Abraham as he rejects idolatry, receives a divine calling, and experiences powerful visions of heaven. Through rich symbolism and deep moral lessons, the text presents Abraham as both a faithful servant of God and an intercessor for humanity.

By including this text in the collection, readers can gain a deeper understanding of Abraham's importance in religious history and the broader spiritual ideas of ancient Judaism.

Abraham was known for his kindness, fairness, and generosity. He lived near a place called Dria the Black, at a crossroads where many travelers passed through. He welcomed everyone—rich or poor, kings or commoners, strong or weak. No matter who they were, Abraham treated them with kindness because he was a good and just man who loved people.

One day, the Lord called the archangel Michael and said, "Go to my servant Abraham and remind him that his time on earth is coming to an end. I have blessed him greatly, making his descendants as countless as the stars in the sky and the sand on the shore. He has lived a life full of goodness and generosity. Now, his time has come."

Michael, who sat before the Lord, left heaven and went to find Abraham in Dria the Black. When he arrived, he saw Abraham working in the field with his servants and some young men. The archangel approached him and said, "Greetings, honored father, chosen one of the Lord, beloved friend of the King of Heaven."

Abraham replied, "Greetings to you, mighty one of God's army! You are more radiant than any man I have ever seen. Tell me, young man, where do you come from, and why do you shine so brightly?"

Michael answered, "Righteous Abraham, I come from the Great City. The Great King has sent me to His chosen friend to tell him to prepare himself, for the Lord is calling him."

Abraham nodded and said, "Very well. Let us go back to my home." Then he called his servants and said, "Go to the field and bring two of my horses. Prepare them so I may ride one, and my guest may ride the other."

But Michael replied, "Do not bring the horses. I do not ride animals with four legs. Let us walk together, righteous one."

As they walked, they passed by a tall and sturdy cypress tree. Suddenly, the tree cried out, "The Lord calls you, Abraham!" But Abraham remained silent, unsure if the angel had heard it.

When they reached Abraham's home, they sat down. Isaac, Abraham's son, saw the angel and said to his mother, Sarah, "Look at the man sitting with my father. He does not look like any ordinary person."

Isaac ran to the angel, bowed before him, and the angel blessed him, saying, "May God give you all the blessings He has given to your father and mother."

Abraham turned to Isaac and said, "Bring a basin and fill it with water so we can wash our guest's feet."

Isaac ran to the well, filled a basin, and brought it back. As Abraham washed the angel's feet, he sighed deeply and began to cry. Seeing his father weep, Isaac also started to cry, and their tears fell together. The angel, moved by their sadness, wept as well. As his tears fell into the basin, they turned into precious stones.

When Abraham saw this, he gathered the jewels and kept their meaning in his heart.

Then Abraham told his son, "Go prepare two beds carefully. Set candles in the candlesticks, lay out the table, light incense, and spread fragrant herbs on the floor so the room smells sweet. Light seven candles so that we may celebrate this guest, who is greater than any man and mightier than kings."

Isaac did everything as his father instructed.

Abraham and the angel went into the prepared room. They sat down on separate beds with a table of food between them. Then the angel returned to the Lord and said, "Lord, I have seen Abraham's righteousness, kindness, and incredible strength. I cannot bring myself to tell him about his approaching death because I have never met anyone like him on earth."

The Lord replied, "Go back to my friend Abraham. Eat the food he has prepared, and I will send My Spirit to his son Isaac. In a dream, I will reveal to him that his father's time is near. You will interpret the dream so that Abraham may understand that his time has come."

The archangel said, "Lord, heavenly beings do not eat or drink. How can I sit and eat with Abraham?"

The Lord replied, "Do not worry. I will send spirits to make the food disappear from your hands and mouth, as if you were eating. This will bring joy to Abraham and his family. Also, explain Isaac's dream so they understand what is about to happen."

The archangel returned to Abraham, and they ate together. As usual, Abraham said a prayer before the meal. After eating, they prayed again and then rested on their beds.

Isaac turned to his father and said, "I want to stay here and listen to our guest."

But Abraham replied, "No, my son. Go to bed and rest. We must not trouble our guest."

Isaac obeyed, received his father's blessing, and went to his room.

Later that night, Isaac had a dream that frightened him. He ran to his father's room, where Abraham was still with the archangel, and cried, "Father Abraham, please open the door! Let me hold you before they take you away from me!"

Abraham got up and opened the door. Isaac ran inside, embraced his father, and wept loudly. Abraham also wept, and when the archangel saw them, he wept too.

Abraham gently asked Isaac, "My dear son, tell me what you saw in your dream that has upset you so much."

Isaac replied, "I saw the sun and the moon resting on my head, shining brightly in all directions. At first, I was happy, but then the heavens opened, and a glowing man came down. He removed the sun from my head and took it to heaven. Then he did the same with the moon. I begged him, 'Please, do not take them away from me!' But he said, 'Let them go. The Lord of Heaven has called for them.' Although they left some of their light behind, I felt heartbroken."

Abraham sighed and said, "The sun you saw, and the glowing man from heaven, must mean that my time to leave has come." He then turned to the angel and said, "Oh, how amazing! But I fear you are the one who has come to take my soul from me."

The archangel replied, "I am the angel sent to bring you news of your passing. You will go to the Lord as promised in your covenant."

Abraham answered, "Now I understand that you are here to take my soul, but I will not go willingly!"

The angel returned to the Lord and reported everything that had happened, including Abraham's refusal, saying, "He will not surrender."

The Lord said to the archangel, "Go back to my friend Abraham and remind him: I am the Lord, his God, who led him to the Promised Land. I blessed him with descendants as countless as the sand on the shore and the stars in the sky. How dare he resist me? Does he not know that since the time of Adam and Eve, all people have died? Kings, ancestors, and all of humanity have faced death because no one is immortal.

"But I have not sent him sickness, suffering, or the grim reaper to take him away. Instead, I sent my archangel Michael with this message so Abraham could prepare himself. Why does he resist my messenger? Does he not know I could send the angel of death, whose presence he could not endure?"

The archangel returned to Abraham and repeated the Lord's words. Abraham wept and said, "Mighty angel of heaven, though I am a sinner, you have honored me. Please grant me one last request. The Lord has always answered my prayers and given me what I asked for. I know I cannot escape death, but before I die, let me see all the people of the earth and their deeds while I am still alive. After that, I will surrender myself completely."

The archangel returned to heaven and told the Lord about

Abraham's request.

The Lord said, "Place my servant Abraham in the chariot of the cherubim and bring him up to heaven."

Then sixty angels prepared the chariot. Abraham was lifted up on the clouds. As he traveled, he saw another chariot behind him and groups of people below.

In one area, he saw people committing terrible sins and cried out, "Lord, let the earth open and swallow them!"

In another place, he saw people stealing and harming others and shouted, "Lord, send fire from heaven to destroy them!"

Fire came down and consumed them.

A voice from heaven commanded, "Take Abraham away from this sight so he will not see the people any longer. If he continues watching their sins, he will destroy them all. But I do not wish for anyone to perish. I want the wicked to repent and live. Take Abraham to the first gate of heaven so he may witness the final judgment and humble himself even more."

The archangel turned Abraham's chariot and brought him to the first gate of heaven. There, he saw two paths—one narrow and difficult, the other wide and easy.

On the narrow path, only a few souls were walking, each guided by an angel.

On the wide path, there were many souls, but they looked wounded and suffering, being led by different beings.

Then Abraham noticed a powerful figure sitting on a golden throne. Sometimes, the figure wept, pulling at his hair and beard when he saw the many souls on the wide path. Other times, he rejoiced when he saw the few souls walking the narrow path.

Abraham turned to the archangel and asked, "Who is this man who switches between sorrow and joy?"

The archangel answered, "This is Adam, the first man, created to bring beauty to the world. He rejoices when he sees souls on the narrow path because it leads to life. But when he sees so many souls on the wide path, which leads to destruction, he mourns deeply."

As they spoke, two angels arrived, bringing countless souls before Adam. Some were sent down the narrow path, while others were turned away.

Then Abraham saw another golden throne at a large gateway. It shined like fire, and a man sat on it, resembling the Son of God. In front of him was a massive table, and two angels stood beside him.

One angel held a set of scales, and the other held a scroll listing all the temptations and sins of humanity. The man judged each soul, deciding their fate.

The angel on the right recorded virtues, while the angel on the left noted sins. Some souls were condemned, others were set free, and a few were placed in the middle.

Abraham asked the archangel, "What is this I see before me?"

The angel replied, "These are the judges, and they pass judgment on every soul that comes before them."

Abraham watched as one soul was brought forward.

An angel said, "This soul has an equal number of good and bad deeds. Erase its record, for it will neither be saved nor condemned. Place it in the middle."

Abraham then asked, "Who are these judges and the glowing angels surrounding them?"

The archangel said, "Lord, heavenly beings do not eat or drink. How can I sit and eat with Abraham?"

The Lord replied, "Do not worry. I will send spirits to make the food disappear from your hands and mouth, as if you were eating. This will bring joy to Abraham and his family. Also, explain Isaac's dream so they understand what is about to happen."

The archangel returned to Abraham, and they ate together. As usual, Abraham said a prayer before the meal. After eating, they prayed again and then rested on their beds.

Isaac turned to his father and said, "I want to stay here and listen to our guest."

But Abraham replied, "No, my son. Go to bed and rest. We must not trouble our guest."

Isaac obeyed, received his father's blessing, and went to his room.

Later that night, Isaac had a dream that frightened him. He ran to his father's room, where Abraham was still with the archangel, and cried, "Father Abraham, please open the door! Let me hold you before they take you away from me!"

Abraham got up and opened the door. Isaac ran inside, embraced his father, and wept loudly. Abraham also wept, and when the archangel saw them, he wept too.

Abraham gently asked Isaac, "My dear son, tell me what you saw in your dream that has upset you so much."

Isaac replied, "I saw the sun and the moon resting on my head, shining brightly in all directions. At first, I was happy, but then the heavens opened, and a glowing man came down. He removed the sun from my head and took it to heaven. Then he did the same with the moon. I begged him, 'Please, do not take them away from me!' But he said, 'Let them go. The Lord of Heaven has called for them.' Although they left some of their light behind, I felt heartbroken."

Abraham sighed and said, "The sun you saw, and the glowing man from heaven, must mean that my time to leave has come." He then turned to the angel and said, "Oh, how amazing! But I fear you are the one who has come to take my soul from me."

The archangel replied, "I am the angel sent to bring you news of your passing. You will go to the Lord as promised in your covenant."

Abraham answered, "Now I understand that you are here to take my soul, but I will not go willingly!"

The angel returned to the Lord and reported everything that had happened, including Abraham's refusal, saying, "He will not surrender."

The Lord said to the archangel, "Go back to my friend Abraham and remind him: I am the Lord, his God, who led him to the Promised Land. I blessed him with descendants as countless as the sand on the shore and the stars in the sky. How dare he resist me? Does he not know that since the time of Adam and Eve, all people have died? Kings, ancestors, and all of humanity have faced death because no one is immortal.

"But I have not sent him sickness, suffering, or the grim reaper to take him away. Instead, I sent my archangel Michael with this message so Abraham could prepare himself. Why does he resist my messenger? Does he not know I could send the angel of death, whose presence he could not endure?"

The archangel returned to Abraham and repeated the Lord's words. Abraham wept and said, "Mighty angel of heaven, though I am a sinner, you have honored me. Please grant me one last request. The Lord has always answered my prayers and given me what I asked for. I know I cannot escape death, but before I die, let me see all the people of the earth and their deeds while I am still alive. After that, I will surrender myself completely."

The archangel returned to heaven and told the Lord about Abraham's request.

The Lord said, "Place my servant Abraham in the chariot of the cherubim and bring him up to heaven."

Then sixty angels prepared the chariot. Abraham was lifted up on the clouds. As he traveled, he saw another chariot behind him and groups of people below.

In one area, he saw people committing terrible sins and cried out, "Lord, let the earth open and swallow them!"

In another place, he saw people stealing and harming others and shouted, "Lord, send fire from heaven to destroy them!"

Fire came down and consumed them.

A voice from heaven commanded, "Take Abraham away from this sight so he will not see the people any longer. If he continues watching their sins, he will destroy them all. But I do not wish for anyone to perish. I want the wicked to repent and live. Take Abraham to the first gate of heaven so he may witness the final judgment and humble himself even more."

The archangel turned Abraham's chariot and brought him to the first gate of heaven. There, he saw two paths—one narrow and difficult, the other wide and easy.

On the narrow path, only a few souls were walking, each guided by an angel.

On the wide path, there were many souls, but they looked wounded and suffering, being led by different beings.

Then Abraham noticed a powerful figure sitting on a golden throne. Sometimes, the figure wept, pulling at his hair and beard when he saw the many souls on the wide path. Other times, he rejoiced when he saw the few souls walking the narrow path.

Abraham turned to the archangel and asked, "Who is this man who switches between sorrow and joy?"

The archangel answered, "This is Adam, the first man, created to bring beauty to the world. He rejoices when he sees souls on the narrow path because it leads to life. But when he sees so many souls on the wide path, which leads to destruction, he mourns deeply."

As they spoke, two angels arrived, bringing countless souls before Adam. Some were sent down the narrow path, while others were turned away.

Then Abraham saw another golden throne at a large gateway. It shined like fire, and a man sat on it, resembling the Son of God. In front of him was a massive table, and two angels stood beside him.

One angel held a set of scales, and the other held a scroll listing all the temptations and sins of humanity. The man judged each soul, deciding their fate.

The angel on the right recorded virtues, while the angel on the left noted sins. Some souls were condemned, others were set free, and a few were placed in the middle.

Abraham asked the archangel, "What is this I see before me?"

The angel replied, "These are the judges, and they pass judgment on every soul that comes before them."

Abraham watched as one soul was brought forward.

An angel said, "This soul has an equal number of good and bad deeds. Erase its record, for it will neither be saved nor condemned. Place it in the middle."

Abraham then asked, "Who are these judges and the glowing angels surrounding them?"

The Vision of Ezra

Introduction

The Vision of Ezra is an ancient text that describes what happens after death, showing the rewards of the righteous and the punishments of the wicked. It is written as a series of visions experienced by Ezra, also known as Salathiel.

Although the text claims that Ezra wrote it, scholars believe it was actually written sometime between the 2nd and 10th centuries AD. The oldest copies that still exist today are in Latin and date back to the 11th century. However, experts think the original text was written in Greek, suggesting it came from a Hellenistic background. The exact time it was written is unknown, but its style and themes are similar to Christian writings from the 3rd and 4th centuries.

The Vision of Ezra has been found in seven Latin manuscripts from the 11th to the 13th centuries, with important copies stored in the Vatican Library and other monasteries in Austria. The similarities between these copies show that the text was well-known and influential in medieval Christian teachings.

The story follows Ezra on a deep spiritual journey. He asks for the strength to witness God's judgment on sinners, and in response, seven angels guide him through the different levels of punishment. Along the way, he sees:

- Fiery Gates – These are guarded by lions that breathe flames.
- Punishment of Sinners – The wicked suffer in terrifying ways, such as being attacked by wild dogs or burned in fire.

- Reward of the Righteous – Those who have lived well pass safely through fire, which purifies them and prepares them for salvation.

These powerful images highlight the difference between the fate of good and evil people, showing God's justice and mercy.

The Vision of Ezra reflects early Christian beliefs about the afterlife and final judgment. It describes heaven and hell in great detail, offering lessons on morality, repentance, and salvation. The text also emphasizes free will, showing that people's choices in life determine what happens to them after death.

This text has similarities to other apocalyptic writings, such as the Greek Apocalypse of Ezra and 2 Esdras (also called 4 Ezra). All of these focus on visions of the afterlife and divine judgment, but the Vision of Ezra is shorter and tells a more focused story. Its unique feature is Ezra's journey through different spiritual realms, guided by angels.

The Vision of Ezra gives a strong picture of early Christian beliefs about what happens after death, God's judgment, and the choices people make in life. Its detailed descriptions and important lessons still have meaning today, offering a glimpse into the religious and spiritual ideas of the past.

The Book of Ezra The Scribe, Who Is Called Salathiel

Vision I

Introduction (III. I 3).

In the 30th year after our city was destroyed, I, Salathiel, also known as Ezra, was in Babylon. I lay on my bed, feeling troubled, as many thoughts filled my mind. I saw how Zion had been left in ruins while

Babylon's homes were filled with riches. My heart was overwhelmed, and I cried out to God in fear.

I said, "Lord, didn't you speak from the beginning when you created the earth? You alone shaped everything, commanding the dust to form Adam. You breathed life into him, and he became a living being. You placed him in the paradise you had prepared before the earth existed.

You gave him one command, but he disobeyed it. Because of this, you sentenced him and his descendants to death. From him came many nations, tribes, and languages—too many to count. They all followed their own ways, committing evil, but you did not stop them.

Then, in time, you sent a great flood to destroy the people of the world because of their wickedness. They all perished, just as Adam faced death. But you spared one man and his family, and from them, all the righteous people were born.

As people multiplied again, their wickedness grew worse than before. When they turned away from you, you chose one man, Abraham. You loved him and revealed your plans for the future. You made an everlasting covenant with him, promising to never abandon his descendants.

You gave him Isaac, and to Isaac, you gave Jacob and Esau. You chose Jacob's descendants as your own people, while you rejected Esau. Jacob's family grew into a great nation. When you brought them out of Egypt, you renewed your covenant with them and led them to Mount Sinai.

You shook the heavens and the earth, causing the sea to tremble and the world to fear your power. Your glory passed through fire, earthquakes, wind, and cold to give Jacob's descendants your Law and commandments. But even then, you did not remove their sinful hearts.

Because of Adam, sin had taken root, and everyone born after him inherited his weakness. Even with your Law, people still chose evil.

As time passed, you raised up a servant, David, and commanded him to build a city for your name, a place where offerings would be made to you. For many years, this was done. But the people of that city also sinned against you, just as Adam and his descendants had done. They followed their sinful hearts, so you allowed their enemies to take the city.

Seeing this, I wondered in my heart: Are the people of Babylon really better? Have you abandoned Zion for them? Since I arrived here, I have witnessed endless sins. For 30 years, I have seen terrible wrongdoing. My heart is troubled because I see you allow sinners to thrive, while your own people have been destroyed, and your enemies remain untouched.

You have not made it clear how anyone can understand your ways. Has Babylon really done better than Zion? Is there any other nation you favor more than Israel? What other people have kept your covenant like Jacob's descendants? Yet, they have not been rewarded, and their hard work has not paid off.

I have traveled among many nations and seen that they are successful, even though they do not follow your commands. If you weigh our sins against those of the rest of the world, the balance would not tip much in either direction. Have the people of the world ever stopped sinning before you? Has any nation truly obeyed your laws? There may be a few individuals who have followed your commands, but not an entire people.

Then the angel Uriel, who had been sent to me, spoke and said, "Are you so troubled by this world that you wish to understand the ways of the Most High?"

I replied, "Yes, my Lord."

The angel continued, "I have three challenges for you. If you can answer one of them, I will show you the truth about why there is evil in the world."

I said, "Please tell me."

He said, "Weigh fire on a scale, measure the wind, or bring back a day that has already passed."

I answered, "No one born of man could do these things. Why do you ask me something impossible?"

Then he said, "What if I had asked you how many chambers are in the ocean, how many springs flow from underground, or how many paths lead to heaven? Could you answer? You would say you have never gone to the depths of the sea, nor to the underworld, nor have you risen to heaven. But I did not ask about those things. I asked about fire, wind, and time—things you live with every day. And yet, you cannot explain them."

Then he said, "If you cannot understand what happens around you, how can you expect to understand the ways of the Most High? His ways are beyond human understanding. A mortal person living in a corrupt world cannot grasp the wisdom of an eternal God."

When I heard this, I fell to the ground and said, "It would have been better if we had never been born. Now we live in sin, we suffer, and we do not even understand why."

The angel answered, "Let me tell you a story.

"Once, the trees of the forest gathered together and said, 'Let's go to war against the sea so that it will move back and give us more land to grow.'

"But the waves of the sea also gathered together and said, 'Let's go to war against the trees so that we can take their land for the waters.'

"But in the end, fire came and burned the trees, and the sand rose up to stop the waves. Both plans were useless.

"If you had been the judge, who would you say was right and who was wrong?"

I replied, "Neither plan made sense. The trees were meant to stay on the land, and the sea was meant to hold its waves."

Then the angel said, "You have judged correctly! So why do you not judge yourself in the same way? Just as trees belong to the land and waves belong to the sea, people on earth can only understand what happens on earth. Only those in heaven can understand the things above."

I answered, "Then tell me, my Lord, why was I given the ability to think if I cannot understand these things? I am not asking about what is above the heavens. I only want to understand what happens around me every day.

"Why has Israel been handed over to other nations? Why have your chosen people fallen into the hands of those who do not believe in you? Why has the holy Law been ignored? Why have the covenants written for us disappeared?

"We pass from this world like insects, and our lives are as brief as a breath. We do not deserve your mercy, but what will you do for the sake of your great name, which we carry? That is what I want to understand."

The Answer

The angel answered me, "If you live long enough, you will see and be amazed because this world is quickly passing away. It cannot last forever, especially since it is full of suffering and pain. It is not strong enough to hold the great rewards promised to the righteous.

"The evil you asked me about has already been planted, but its time to be harvested has not yet come. Until the evil is removed, the good cannot fully grow. From the very beginning, one seed of evil was planted in Adam's heart, and look at how much sin it has produced over time. And it will continue until the time for the harvest arrives.

"Now, think for yourself—how much wickedness has grown from that one seed? So imagine when countless seeds of goodness are planted—how great will the harvest be?"

I asked, "How long will it take for this to happen? Our lives are short and full of trouble."

The angel replied, "You cannot rush ahead of the Most High. You want things to happen quickly for yourself, but God is waiting for the sake of many. Even the souls of the righteous, who are waiting in their resting places, ask, 'How much longer must we wait? When will we receive our reward?'

"The angel Remiel answered them, saying, 'You must wait until the full number of righteous people has been reached.'

"The Holy One has measured the world carefully. He has counted the times and set the seasons in place. He will not change anything or rush the process until everything is complete."

I said, "Lord, but the world is full of sin! Are the righteous being delayed because of all the evil that people do?"

The angel answered, "Go ask a pregnant woman if she can hold her baby inside her after nine months."

I replied, "No, my Lord, she cannot."

Then he said, "The underworld and the resting places of souls are like a mother's womb. Just as a woman cannot hold back her child when it is time to give birth, the world cannot delay what has been set in motion. When the time comes, everything that has been waiting since the beginning will be revealed."

I asked, "If I have found favor in your eyes, please show me something else. Has more time already passed than what remains? I know about the past, but I do not know what is still ahead."

The angel said, "Stand to my right, and I will show you."

I stood and saw a huge fire burning fiercely. When the flames died down, I saw that smoke remained. Then I saw a heavy storm cloud filled with water, pouring down a violent rain. But after the storm passed, a few drops of water were still left behind.

Then the angel said, "Think about what you saw. Just as the fire was much greater than the smoke, and the rain was heavier than the drops that remained, so too has most of time already passed. Only a little remains."

The Signs Which Precede The End (IV. 51-V.13)

I asked him, "Will I live to see those days? Who will be alive when these things happen?"

He answered, "I can tell you some of the signs you asked about, but I was not sent to tell you about your life. I do not know the answer to that."

"As for the signs," he continued, "the time is coming when people on earth will be overcome with fear. Truth will be hidden, and faith will disappear. Sin and shamelessness will be worse than anything you see now or have heard about in the past.

"The land you see now will become unstable and abandoned. If the Most High allows you to live, you will see the land in total confusion after three days.

"Strange things will happen. The sun will shine at night, and the moon will be bright during the day. Trees will drip blood, and stones will speak. People will be in chaos, and the air will change.

"A ruler will rise whom no one expects, and birds will leave their usual places.

"The sea of Sodom will be full of fish, and a mysterious voice will be heard at night, surprising everyone.

"Cracks will open in many places, and fire will keep bursting out. Wild animals will leave their habitats, and strange things will happen to pregnant women—some babies will not develop fully before birth.

"Fresh water will become salty. Friends will suddenly turn against each other in battle.

"Wisdom will disappear, and understanding will be hidden. People will search for them but will not find them.

"Sin and shamelessness will spread everywhere. People will ask their neighbors, 'Have you seen anyone doing what is right?' But the answer will always be 'No.'

"During that time, people will hope but never receive what they wish for. The land will struggle to produce food, and hard work will not lead to success.

"I was told to share these signs with you. But if you pray again as you have been doing, and fast for seven more days, you will hear even greater things."

The Conclusion of The Vision (V. 14-19)

I woke up, shaking all over, and felt so weak that it seemed like my life was slipping away.

But the angel who had been speaking to me reached out, helped me stand, and gave me strength.

On the second night, Phaltiel, the leader of the people, came to me and asked, "Where have you been? Why do you look so troubled? Don't you know that you have been chosen to care for Israel while they are in captivity?

"Get up and eat something so you don't abandon us, like a shepherd leaving his flock to be attacked by wolves!"

But I told him, "Leave me alone. Do not come near me for seven days. After that, you can return, and I will explain everything to you."

After I said this, he left.

Vision II

The Prayer of Ezra 1

I fasted for seven days, crying and mourning, just as the angel Ramiel had told me to do. After the seven days, my heart was still troubled, and I felt overwhelmed with thoughts. But then, my soul was filled with understanding, and I began to pray again, speaking to the Most High with deep pleading.

I said, "Lord, from all the trees in the world, you have chosen one vine. From all the lands, you have picked one special place. From the deep waters of the sea, you have set aside one river. Among all the flowers, you have chosen one. From all the cities ever built, you made Zion your holy place.

"Among all the birds, you have named one dove as special. From all the animals, you have chosen one sheep. And from all the nations, you have brought one people close to you, giving them the law you approved of and loved.

"But now, Lord, why have you given the chosen one over to so many? Why have you allowed your special people to be scattered among the nations? Those who reject your commandments have trampled on the ones who believed in your covenant. If you were so angry with your people, shouldn't you have punished them yourself instead of letting others destroy them?"

After I finished speaking, the angel who had appeared to me before returned and said, "Listen to me, Ezra, and I will explain. Look at me, and I will give you understanding."

I replied, "Speak, my lord."

The angel asked, "Are you so troubled about Israel? Do you love them more than the One who created them?"

I said, "No, my lord! But my heart is in pain, and I suffer every moment because I want to understand God's judgment."

The angel said, "You cannot understand."

I asked, "Why not, my lord? Why was I even born if I cannot understand these things? Why wasn't my mother's womb my grave so I would not have to see the suffering of Jacob and the pain of Israel's descendants?"

The angel answered, "If you can count the people who have not yet been born, gather the raindrops that have fallen, or make dead flowers bloom again—if you can open doors that have never been unlocked, control the winds that are held back, or show me the face of someone you have never seen—then I will tell you what you want to know."

I replied, "Lord, only the One who does not live among men can know these things. I am weak and foolish—how could I possibly understand what you ask?"

The angel said, "Just as you cannot do any of these things, you also cannot understand God's judgment or the depth of the love He has promised His people."

Then I asked, "Lord, you made promises to those who will live at the end of time. But what about the people who came before us, those who live now, and those who will come after us?"

The angel answered, "God's judgment is fair to all. There is no advantage for those who came first, and no disadvantage for those who come last."

I asked, "But couldn't you have created everyone all at once so that we could all be judged together?"

The angel answered me and said, "Creation does not move faster than its Creator. If everything were created all at once, the world would not be able to support it."

I replied, "But you just told me that all creation will be brought back to life at the same time. If that is true, then why couldn't everything have been made at once from the start?"

The angel responded, "Ask a woman who is pregnant, 'If you carry ten children, why don't you give birth to them all at once?' Demand that she deliver them all at the same time."

I answered, "She cannot, my lord. She can only give birth at the right time."

He said, "In the same way, I have made the earth like a womb, where people come into the world at different times. Just as a newborn child cannot give birth and an old woman can no longer bear children, I have set the world in order."

Then I asked, "Since you have explained this to me, let me ask another question. The city of Zion, which you spoke about—does she still have her strength, or is she growing old?"

The angel said, "Ask a mother who has given birth, and she will tell you. Say to her, 'Why are the children you bear now smaller than those who came before?' She will answer, 'Children born when I was young were strong, but those born when I was old are weaker because my body has aged.'

"In the same way, if you look at the people of today, you will see that they are smaller and weaker than those who lived before them. And the people who come after you will be even weaker because creation itself is growing old, and its strength is fading."

Then I said, "Please, my lord, if I have found favor in your eyes, tell me who will bring the end of the world."

The angel answered, "The beginning was in the hands of men, but the end will come by my own hands.

"Before the land of the world was formed, before the winds blew, before thunder was heard, before lightning flashed, before the garden of Paradise was planted, before the flowers bloomed, before the mighty forces of nature moved, before the angels gathered, before the sky stretched high, before the foundations of Zion were set, before the present time was measured, before people began to sin, and before those with faith were chosen—I had already planned it all. Everything that exists was made by my own hand, not by anyone else."

Then I asked, "What does it mean that time will be divided? When will the first age end and the next one begin?"

The angel answered, "From Abraham to Abraham. Abraham had Isaac, and Isaac had Jacob and Esau. When they were born, Jacob held Esau's heel.

"Esau represents the end of one time, and Jacob represents the beginning of another. Just as a man's life starts with his hand and ends with his heel, time moves in the same way. There is nothing more you need to understand, Ezra."

The Signs of The Last Time and The End

I replied, "Lord, if I have found favor in your eyes, please show me the full meaning of the signs you have revealed to me in part during the night."

The angel answered, "Stand up on your feet, and you will hear a loud voice. If the ground beneath you shakes while you listen, do not be afraid. The voice will be speaking about the end of time, and even the foundations of the earth will understand this message. They will shake and tremble because they will know that their time is changing."

As I listened, I stood up and heard a voice like the sound of rushing waters. It said:

"The time is coming when I will visit those who live on the earth and hold the wicked accountable for their actions. When the suffering of Zion is finished and this world is about to come to an end, I will show these signs:

- The books of judgment will be opened in the sky, and everyone will see my decision.
- One-year-old children will be able to speak.
- Pregnant women will give birth after only three or four months, and their babies will live and move.
- Fields that were once empty will suddenly grow crops.
- Storehouses full of food will suddenly be empty.
- A loud trumpet will sound, and everyone will hear it and be afraid.
- Friends will turn against each other like enemies, and the earth will be shocked by what happens.
- Springs of water will stop flowing for three hours.

Anyone who survives these events will witness my salvation and the end of the world. They will see those who have been taken up and have never experienced death. The hearts and minds of the people will be changed, and they will think differently.

- Evil will be wiped away, and lies will disappear.
- Faith will grow, and corruption will be defeated.
- Truth will finally appear after being hidden for so many years."

As the voice spoke, I felt the ground beneath me begin to shake little by little.

The Conclusion of The Vision (VI. 30-34)

The angel said to me, "I have come to reveal these things to you tonight. If you pray and fast for another seven days, I will show you even greater things.

Your voice has been heard by the Most High. The Mighty One has seen your sincerity and the holiness you have shown since your youth.

That is why He has sent me to reveal these things to you.

Take courage and do not be afraid! But do not be quick to judge the past, or you may be judged in the final days."

Vision III

(Vi. . 35-Ix. 25)

Introduction (VI. 35-37)

After this, I cried and went without food for seven days so I could complete the three weeks I had been told to do. On the eighth night, I felt troubled again, and I spoke to the Most High because my heart was heavy with emotion, and my soul felt like it was burning inside me.

I said, "Lord, you spoke at the beginning of creation and commanded the heavens and earth to exist, and your Word completed the work. Your Spirit moved over everything, while darkness covered all, and no human voice had yet been heard. Then you commanded a ray of light to come from your treasures so that all your works could be seen.

On the second day, you created the sky to separate the waters, placing some above and some below. On the third day, you gathered the waters into one area, revealing dry land. You set aside part of the land to be used for farming and ordered it to produce food. Immediately, all kinds of fruit grew—too many to count—each with its own taste. Beautiful flowers bloomed in many shapes, and trees appeared, each different from the other. Their scents were beyond description. All of this happened on the third day.

On the fourth day, you commanded the sun, moon, and stars to shine and serve mankind, whom you were about to create. On the fifth day, you told the waters to bring forth all kinds of creatures—birds, fish, and animals—so that they would show your wonders. Though the waters had no life of their own, they produced living things. You also created two great creatures: one you called Behemoth, and the other Leviathan. You separated them because the sea could not hold them both together. Behemoth was placed in a dry area with a thousand mountains, while Leviathan was kept in the waters. You have saved them for when you decide they will be used as food.

On the sixth day, you commanded the earth to bring forth land animals, crawling creatures, and livestock. Over all of these, you placed Adam as their ruler, and from him, we, your chosen people, have come.

I have told you all of this, Lord, because you said you created the world for our sake. But as for the other people who also come from Adam, you said they are nothing, like a drop of water from a bucket or spit on the ground. And yet now, these same people rule over us and oppress us! But we, your chosen people, your firstborn and beloved ones, have been given into their hands.

If this world was created for us, then why do we not rule over it? How much longer must we endure this?"

After I finished speaking, the angel who had visited me before came again and said, "Stand up, Ezra, and listen to the words I have come to tell you."

I said, "Speak, my Lord."

He answered, "Imagine a vast sea that is wide and endless, but there is only a narrow entrance, like a river. If someone wants to enter the sea, see it, and take control of it, they must first go through the narrow path. If they do not pass through the narrow way, how can they ever reach the open sea?"

Listen to this example: There is a city built in a wide valley, filled with many good things. However, the entrance to the city is narrow and placed on high ground. On one side, there is fire, and on the other, deep waters.

A single narrow path runs between them, just wide enough for one person to walk at a time. If someone is meant to inherit that city, how can they receive it unless they first pass through the dangers that block the way?

I answered, "That makes sense, my Lord!" And he said to me, "This is also true for Israel. I created the world for them, but when Adam disobeyed my commands, everything was cursed. That is why life in this world is now full of suffering, pain, and danger. But the next world will be wide, peaceful, and full of everlasting goodness.

If people don't go through struggles and hardships, they won't be able to receive what has been prepared for them.

So why are you upset that people are weak and mortal? Why do you focus only on what is happening now instead of looking at what is to come?

I answered, "Lord, you said in your Law that good people will inherit these blessings, but the wicked will be destroyed. The righteous endure hardships because they hope for a greater reward, but the wicked suffer too—and they never get to see the reward!"

He replied, "You are not wiser than God or greater than the Most High! Many will perish because they rejected my Law, which I gave them so they could live. I told them what to do to avoid punishment, but they refused to listen. Instead, they chose to follow empty and worthless thoughts, turned away from the truth, and even denied that the Most High exists.

They rejected his Law, broke his promises, ignored his commands, and refused to acknowledge his works.

So, Ezra, empty things belong to those who are empty, but those who are full will receive what is full."

The Temporary Messianic Kingdom and The End of The World (VP. 26-[44])

The time is coming when the signs I told you about will happen. The bride, who has been hidden, will appear like a great city, and what was once cut off will be seen again.

Anyone who survives these troubles will witness my wonders.

My son, the Messiah, will be revealed, along with those who are with him, and they will bring joy to those who remain for thirty years. After that time, my son, the Messiah, will die, along with all people who are still living. Then, for seven days, the world will return to the silence it had in the beginning, and no one will be left.

After those seven days, the world will wake up again, and corruption will be destroyed. The earth will give up the dead, the dust will release those buried in it, and the hidden places will return the souls that were placed there. The Most High will sit on the throne of judgment, and the end will come. Mercy will be no more, and patience will be gone. Only my judgment will remain. Truth will stand, and faith will grow.

The good and evil deeds of all people will be revealed. The spirit of torment will appear, but so will the place of rest. The fires of Gehenna will be shown, but across from it will be the paradise of peace.

Then the Most High will say to the nations, "Look at what you have rejected! See the one you refused to serve and the commands you ignored! Look before you—on one side, rest and joy; on the other, fire and suffering!" That is how he will speak on the Day of Judgment.

On that day, the sun, moon, and stars will not shine. There will be no clouds, lightning, or thunder. The wind, water, and air will not move. There will be no darkness, no morning or evening, no summer or winter. There will be no heat, cold, frost, hail, dew, or rain. Time itself—day and night—will no longer exist. There will be no lamps, no torches, no light, except for the shining glory of the Most High. From that light, people will see what has been decided for them.

There will be a waiting period, like a week of years, but this is part of the plan. I have revealed it only to you.

I answered and said, "Lord, I have said before and I say again: Blessed are those who have lived and obeyed your commands. But what about those I prayed for? Is there anyone who has lived without sin? Is there anyone born who has never disobeyed your command?

Now I see that few will find joy in the world to come, but many will face suffering.

For inside us is an evil heart that leads us away from the right path. It drags us into corruption and shows us the way to death. It leads us far from life, and this has happened not just to a few, but to nearly everyone who has ever lived."

The angel answered me and said, "Listen, Ezra, and I will explain things to you again.

The Most High did not create just one world, but two. You asked why there are so few righteous people, so let me give you an example.

If you had a few precious stones, would you compare them to piles of lead and clay?

I asked, "How does that make sense, Lord?"

And he replied, "Ask the earth, and she will tell you. Speak to her, and she will explain. The earth produces gold, silver, copper, iron, lead, and clay. But silver is more common than gold, copper is more common than silver, iron is more common than copper, lead is more common than iron, and clay is the most common of all. Now, tell me, what is more valuable—the rare things or the abundant ones?"

I answered, "Lord, the things that are rare are the most precious, while the things that are common have little value."

Then he said to me, "Now think about what you just said. People rejoice more over a small amount of something valuable than over an abundance of something worthless. The same is true for my judgment. I take joy in the few who live righteously because they bring glory to my name. But I do not grieve over the many who perish, because they are like a breath of air, like smoke that vanishes, like a flame that burns out and disappears."

Then I cried out, "Oh, earth, what have you done? You have brought forth people who are now doomed to destruction! If human intelligence comes from the dust like everything else, then it would have been better if the dust had never existed, so that intelligence would never have been born.

But now, intelligence grows within us, and that is why we suffer—because we understand what is happening, yet we still perish!

Let the human race mourn, but let the animals of the field rejoice! Let all who are born weep, but let the cattle and sheep celebrate! It is better for them than for us, because they do not fear judgment, they do not know punishment, and they were never promised life after death.

So what good is it for us to live, only to suffer?

Every person is born into sin, burdened with wrongdoing from the start. If we did not have to face judgment after death, it would be better for us!"

Then the angel answered me and said, "When the Most High created the world, Adam, and all who came after him, he also prepared judgment and everything that comes with it.

Now think about your own words—you said that intelligence grows within people. That is exactly why they must face judgment! They had understanding, yet they chose to do evil. They received commandments but did not follow them. The Law was given to them, but they rejected it.

What will they say on the day of judgment? How will they defend themselves when the time comes?

For so long, the Most High has been patient with the people of this world—not for their sake, but because the right time had to come."

The State of The Soul Between Death and Judgement VII.

I asked, "Lord, if I have found favor with you, please tell me this: After we die and our souls leave our bodies, do we rest until the time comes when you renew the world, or do we immediately face torment?"

He answered, "I will explain this to you, but do not associate yourself with those who rebel or suffer punishment. You have stored up good deeds with the Most High, and your reward will be revealed at the appointed time.

As for death, here is what happens: When a person's time to die comes, as determined by the Most High, their spirit leaves their body and returns to the One who gave it. First, the soul acknowledges the glory of God.

But if the soul belonged to someone who denied God, rejected His ways, or hated those who feared Him, it does not enter a place of rest. Instead, it immediately suffers torment in seven ways:

1. They realize they have disobeyed the law of the Most High.

2. They understand they can no longer repent or do good deeds to save themselves.

3. They see the reward given to those who were faithful.

4. They recognize the punishment waiting for them in the end and regret not following God when they had the chance.

5. They look upon the peaceful rest of the righteous souls, knowing they will never experience it.

6. They see the suffering prepared for them and know it is unavoidable.

7. Worst of all, they are consumed with shame and fear as they see the glory of the Most High, the one they disobeyed in life, and they know they will face His judgment.

But for those who have followed the ways of the Most High, this is what happens when their time comes:

While they were alive, they faithfully served God, enduring struggles and hardships to keep His commandments. Because of this, when they die, they experience seven great joys:

1. They rejoice in the victory of overcoming evil desires and staying on the path of life.

2. They see the suffering of the wicked and realize they have been saved from it.

3. They hear the Most High Himself testify that they have been faithful to His law.

4. They rest peacefully in the chambers of the righteous, guarded by angels, and they see the glorious future that awaits them.

5. They celebrate their escape from the struggles of the world, knowing they now inherit an eternal reward.

6. They see how their faces will shine like the sun and how they will become like the stars, never again to experience corruption.

7. Above all, they feel fearless and confident as they prepare to stand before the One they served in life, knowing they will be honored and rewarded by Him.

These are the paths of the righteous after death, but the disobedient will only know suffering. Their souls do not enter a place of peace but remain in torment, grieving and regretting their choices in seven ways.

Then I asked, "After the soul leaves the body, is there a time when it sees these things you have described?"

He answered me, saying, "For seven days after death, souls are free to see these things I have told you about. After that, they are gathered into their resting places."

Then I asked, "If I have found favor with you, please tell me—on the Day of Judgment, will the righteous be able to pray for the wicked or ask the Most High to have mercy on them? Can fathers pray for their sons, or sons for their fathers? Can brothers, relatives, or friends plead for one another?"

He replied, "Since you have been shown favor, I will explain this as well. The Day of Judgment is final and will reveal the truth to all. Just as no one can take another's sickness, hunger, or suffering in their place—whether a father, a son, a master, or a friend—so too, on that day, no one can pray for another. Each person will carry the weight of their own righteousness or sin."

I said, "But Lord, in the past, Abraham prayed for the people of Sodom. Moses prayed for our ancestors in the wilderness when they sinned. Joshua prayed for Israel after Achan's wrongdoing. Samuel prayed in the time of Saul, and David for the suffering of the people. Solomon prayed for those in the Temple. Elijah prayed for rain and even for the dead to come back to life. Hezekiah prayed for the people when Sennacherib attacked. Many have prayed for others before—so why can't this happen on the Day of Judgment?"

He answered, "This world has an end, and God's glory does not remain in it forever. That is why the strong have prayed for the weak. But the Day of Judgment is different. It is the end of this world and the beginning of the next, which will never die. In that world, corruption will be gone, wickedness will be destroyed, and faithlessness will be no more. Righteousness will flourish, and truth will shine. On that day, no one will be able to help those who are condemned, just as no one can harm those who are saved."

The Promises Of Future Felicity Only Mock A Sin-Stained Race (VII. [N6]-[131])

I answered, "This is my final thought: It would have been better if the earth had never created Adam, or if, when he was created, you had taught him not to sin.

"What good has it done for people to live in suffering, only to die and face punishment? Oh, Adam, what have you done? You were the one who sinned, but the consequences were not just yours—they became ours too, because we came from you!

"What is the point of being promised eternal life when our actions lead to death? What good is it to be given hope that never fades, when we are trapped in misery? What benefit is there in knowing that places of safety and healing exist if we have lived wickedly?

"We are told that the glory of the Most High will protect those who lived righteously, but we chose to follow evil instead. Paradise, filled with fruit that never withers, joy, and healing, has been revealed, but we cannot enter it because of our sinful ways. The faces of the holy will shine brighter than the stars, but our faces will be covered in darkness.

"When we were alive and doing wrong, we never stopped to think about the suffering we would face after death."

He answered me, saying, "This is the challenge that every person faces in life. If they fail, they will suffer, just as you have said. But if they overcome it, they will receive the rewards I have described.

"This is the same message that Moses gave to the people while he was alive. He told them, 'I have set before you today life and death, good and evil. Choose life, so that you and your children may live.'

"But they refused to listen to him. They ignored the prophets who came after him. And even now, they do not believe what I am telling them.

"So, there should be no sadness over their destruction, just as there is joy over those who have chosen life."

Will The Merciful and Compassionate One Suffer So Many to Perish? (VII. [132.]-VIII. 3)

I answered and said, "Lord, I understand that the Most High is called compassionate because he shows kindness even to those who have not yet been born.

"He is called gracious because he welcomes those who turn to his law.

"He is patient because he gives us, his creation, time even when we sin.

"He is generous because he prefers to give rather than take.

"He is full of mercy because he offers kindness not just to those who are alive now, but also to those who have passed and those who are yet to come.

"If he did not show such great mercy, neither the world nor its people would be able to survive.

"He is generous because, in his goodness, he lessens the punishment of sinners—otherwise, hardly one in ten thousand people would still be alive.

"He is also a judge, because if he did not forgive those he created and overlook many of their sins, only a very small number of people would remain."

Viii. R. And He Answered And Said To Me: This World Hath The Most High Made For The Sake Of Many, But That Which Is To Come For The Sake Of Few.

I will share a parable with you, Ezra. If you ask the earth what it produces more of—ordinary clay or precious gold—it will tell you that common dust is far more abundant than gold. The same is true for this world: many people are created, but only a few truly live.

I answered and said, "Let my soul seek understanding, and let my heart gain wisdom! We come into this world without choosing to, and we leave it without wanting to. We are only given a short time to live.

Lord, if you allow me, I will pray to you. Please give us new hearts that can grow good and lasting things so that those who are weak and temporary can have life.

You are the one and only Creator, and we are the work of your hands, as you have said. In the womb, you form our bodies and shape our features. You protect us in warmth and water for nine months until we are born.

The mother's body nourishes the child as you intended, providing milk to help it grow. You guide us with your kindness, sustain us with justice, and teach us through your wisdom. You give us life, and when the time comes, you take it away.

But if you destroy what you took such care to create, what was the purpose of making us in the first place?

I am speaking about all people, but even more, I am speaking about your chosen people. It breaks my heart to see their suffering, and I grieve for the people of Israel.

Now, I will begin to pray for myself and for others, because I see how much we have sinned in this world. I have also heard about the coming judgment. So, please, Lord my God, listen to my prayer as I speak to you.

Translated by Tim Zengerink

The Seer's Prayer for The Divine Compassion on His People.

The prayer of Ezra before he was taken up:

Lord, you live forever, your throne has no limits, and your glory is beyond understanding. The mighty ones stand in fear before you, and at your command, they turn into fire and wind. Your words are true and unchanging, your commands are powerful, and your voice is terrifying.

You can dry up the deep waters with just a look, and your rebuke can make mountains melt. Your truth is clear for all to see. Please listen to your servant's voice, hear my prayer, and pay attention to my words.

As long as I live, I will speak, and as long as I have understanding, I will call out to you. Please do not focus on the sins of your people, but remember those who have served you faithfully. Do not hold onto the foolish actions of the wicked, but think of those who have kept your promises, even when they were treated with shame.

Do not judge those who have done evil before you, but remember those who have feared you with sincerity. Do not destroy those who have acted like animals, but instead look upon those who have followed the light of your law. Do not stay angry with those who have behaved worse than beasts, but love those who have always trusted in your glory.

We, along with those who came before us, have done wrong and acted foolishly. Yet because of our sins, you are called the Compassionate One. If you are willing to show mercy to us, even though we have no good deeds to offer, you will be known as the Gracious One.

The righteous who have done good already have their rewards stored with you. But what is a person that you should be so angry with them? Why be so harsh with a mortal race?

The truth is, there is no one who has not sinned, no one who has lived without doing wrong. So, Lord, let your kindness be known by showing mercy to those who have no good works to offer.

The Divine Reply

And he answered me, saying: Some of the things you have said are correct, and they will happen as you have spoken.

I do not focus on those who do evil, their death, their judgment, or their destruction. Instead, I take joy in the creation of the righteous, in their lives, and in the rewards they will receive.

For as you have said, so it will be.

Mankind Is Like Seed Sown (VIII. 41-45)

Just as a farmer plants many seeds and grows many plants, not all of them survive or take root. In the same way, not everyone who is born will live.

And I answered, "Lord, if I have found favor in your sight, may I ask something? A farmer's seeds will not grow unless they receive rain at the right time, and too much rain can even destroy them. But people are different—they were made by your own hands, in your own image, and you created everything for their sake. How can they be compared to seeds?

Please, Lord, have mercy on your people. Show kindness to your creation, for they belong to you, and you are full of compassion."

The Final Reply; Let The Seer Contemplate the Lot of The Blessed Which He Is Destined to Share (VIII. 46 62)

And he answered me, saying:

"The things of this world belong to those who live in it now, and the things of the future are for those who will come later. You cannot love my creation more than I do. But you have compared yourself to the wicked too many times—do not do this!

However, you will be honored before the Most High because you have humbled yourself, as you should, and have not tried to place yourself among the righteous. Because of this, you will be given even greater honor.

In the end, those who live on the earth will suffer greatly because of their pride. But instead of worrying about them, think about yourself and ask about the rewards of those who are like you.

For you, Paradise is open, the Tree of Life is planted, and the future world is prepared. A place of joy is waiting, a city has been built, and a peaceful rest has been set aside. All that is good has been made complete, and wisdom has reached its fullness. Evil has been locked away, sickness will no longer exist, death will disappear, the grave will be forgotten, and pain will be no more.

In the end, the treasures of life will be revealed. So do not ask again about those who will perish, because they were given freedom, but they rejected the Most High.

They scorned his law and worked to remove his ways from the earth. They even mistreated his faithful ones and said in their hearts, 'There is no God,' even though they knew they would die one day.

Just as the rewards I told you about are waiting for the righteous, suffering and torment are also prepared for the wicked. The Most High never wanted people to be destroyed, but they dishonored his name and refused to be grateful. They rejected the one who gave them life.

And so, my judgment is near. This is something I have not revealed to many people, but only to you and a few like you."

IX. The Signs of The End Reviewed (VIII. 63-IX. 63.

And I said, "Lord, you have shown me many signs of what will happen in the last days, but you haven't told me when it will happen."

He answered, "Pay close attention and think carefully. When you see that some of these signs have already happened, you will know that the Most High is preparing to visit the world He created.

When you notice earthquakes, crowds in chaos, people plotting against each other, leaders struggling for power, and rulers in confusion, understand that these are the events the Most High spoke about long ago.

Just like everything in the world has a clear beginning and end, the times set by the Most High are also known. Their beginnings come with warnings and signs of power, and their end will bring judgment and more signs.

Anyone who survives or escapes—whether through their actions or through their faith—will be safe from the dangers I have described. They will see my salvation in the land I have set apart forever.

But those who ignored my ways will be shocked, and those who rejected and abandoned them will suffer.

All who refused to recognize me while they were alive, even when I was kind to them, and all who rejected my laws while they had the freedom to follow them, will realize the truth after death.

The Fewness of The Saved Further Justified

So don't focus on how the wicked will be punished. Instead, think about how the righteous will live—the ones for whom this world was created.

I replied, "I keep saying, and I will say it again, that more people will be lost than saved. It's like comparing the vast ocean waves to a tiny drop of water."

He answered, "Just as the land determines the kind of seeds that grow, and flowers decide their own colors, and work produces different smells, everything follows a pattern. The farmer's field matches his efforts.

Before people even existed, I had already prepared a place for them to live. No one could stop me—because no one was there yet.

Now that they are here, living in a stable world with everything they need and a law they cannot fully understand, they have become corrupt in their actions. I looked at my world and saw that it was ruined. I saw my creation and realized it was in danger because of the way people behaved.

So I decided to spare only a few. I saved one grape from a whole bunch and one plant from an entire forest.

Let the many be destroyed, since they were created for nothing. But let my chosen ones remain, for they are precious and took great effort to bring into existence.

Conclusion Of The Vision

If you separate yourself for seven more days—but this time, do not fast—go to an open field full of flowers, where no buildings have been built. Eat only the flowers from the field. Do not eat meat or drink wine, only the flowers.

Pray with deep devotion to the Most High, and I will come to you and speak with you.

INTRODUCTION (IX. 26-28)

I went to the field called Arpad, just as he told me, and sat among the flowers. I ate the plants from the field, and they satisfied me.

After seven days, as I lay on the grass, I felt something stir in my heart again, just like before. Then my mouth opened, and I began to speak to the Most High.

The Glory of The Law and Israel; A Contrast (IX. 29-37)

And I said, "Lord, you truly showed yourself to our ancestors in the wilderness when they left Egypt. They traveled through a barren land where nothing grew and no one had ever lived.

You spoke to them, saying, 'Listen to me, Israel, and pay attention, descendants of Jacob! I am planting my Law within you, and it will grow and produce good things. Through it, you will be honored forever.'

But our ancestors received the Law and did not follow it. They were given commandments but did not obey them. The Law itself never faded because it belongs to you, but those who received it perished because they failed to live by it.

It's like how the earth receives seeds, or the sea holds a ship, or a container is filled with food—these things may be used up or destroyed, but what holds them remains. But for us, it has been different.

We received the Law, yet because of our sins, we are destroyed along with our hearts that once accepted it.

Still, your Law does not fade away. It remains in its full glory."

The Vision of The Disconsolate Woman (IX. 38–X. 24)

As I was thinking about these things, I looked up and saw a woman on my right. She was crying loudly, deeply distressed, and sighing in sorrow. Her clothes were torn, and she had thrown dust on her head in grief.

I stopped thinking about my own concerns and turned to her, asking, "Why are you weeping? What is causing you such deep pain?"

She replied, "Please, my lord, allow me to cry freely and continue to grieve, for my heart is filled with sorrow, and I feel completely broken."

I said, "Tell me what has happened to you."

She answered, "I was unable to have children. For thirty years, I was married but could not conceive. Every single day and night, I prayed to the Most High, begging for a child.

Then, after those thirty years, God finally heard my prayers. He saw my suffering, understood my pain, and blessed me with a son.

I was overjoyed. My husband, my neighbors, and I all celebrated and praised the Mighty One. I raised my son with great effort and love.

When he grew up, I arranged for him to be married and planned a joyful wedding feast. But on the night of his wedding, as he entered his new home, he suddenly collapsed and died.

In my grief, I put out the lights, and the people in my town came to comfort me. But I remained silent, waiting until the next day and through the night.

Once everyone was asleep and thought I was resting too, I got up in the darkness, ran away, and came to this field where you see me now.

I have decided that I will never return to the city. I will not eat or drink, but I will continue to mourn and fast until I die."

I let go of my own thoughts and, in my frustration, said to her, "You are being more foolish than any other woman! Can't you see the suffering around us? Do you not realize what has happened to all of us?

Look at Zion, the mother of us all—she is in deep sorrow and has been humiliated beyond measure.

Yes, you grieve for your one son, but we grieve for an entire world in mourning.

Ask the earth, and she will tell you—she has witnessed the birth of countless people, and every one of them, from the beginning of time until now, has passed away. Many more will come, and they too will face destruction.

Who, then, should grieve more? You, for your one son, or the earth, which has lost countless lives?

And if you say, 'My grief is different because I lost the child I carried in my womb, the one I gave birth to and raised with love and hardship,'

Remember that the earth, just like a mother, has brought forth all of humanity. Every person who has ever lived was born from the earth, and all return to it.

So now, keep your sorrow within you. Face your pain with strength, and endure the hardship that has come upon you!"

If you accept the Most High's judgment as fair, then one day, you will be reunited with your son and be honored among women.

So go back to the city, return to your husband.

But she replied, "I will not go back. I will not return to the city or to my husband. I will stay here and die."

I continued speaking to her, saying, "No, don't do this! Instead, think about Zion's suffering and take comfort in Jerusalem's sorrow.

Look at what has happened—our sacred places are destroyed, our altars torn down, our Temple ruined. Our worship has ended, our songs have stopped, and our joy has faded. The light of our lamp has gone out, the ark of the covenant has been taken, and our holy places have been defiled.

The name we carry has been dishonored, our leaders have been shamed, our priests burned, and our Levites taken as prisoners. Our young women have been violated, our wives have been abused, our prophets captured, our watchmen scattered, our children enslaved, and our strongest warriors have been brought low.

And worst of all—the very symbol of Zion's glory has been taken away and handed over to those who hate us.

So let go of your overwhelming grief. Turn to the Mighty One so He may have mercy on you, and the Most High may give you rest from all your suffering."

Sion's Glory; The Vision of The Heavenly Jerusalem (X. 25 28)

As I was speaking with her, her face suddenly began to shine brightly, like a flash of lightning. I was terrified and too afraid to go near her, my heart filled with shock and confusion.

As I tried to understand what was happening, she suddenly let out a loud, terrifying cry, so powerful that the entire earth seemed to shake at the sound of her voice.

Then, as I looked again, she was gone. In her place, I saw a great city with strong, deep foundations. Fear took hold of me, and I cried out,

"Where is the angel Uriel, who has been with me since the beginning? He is the one who led me into this overwhelming experience. Now, I feel lost, my body weak, and my prayers seem worthless."

The Vision Interpreted (X. 29-57)

As I lay on the ground, feeling as if I were dead, the angel who had spoken to me before returned. He saw me there, weak and confused, and took my right hand. He helped me stand up and gave me strength. Then he asked,

"What is troubling you? Why are you so disturbed? Why is your mind so overwhelmed?"

I replied, "Because you left me! I did everything you told me—I went into the field, and I saw something beyond my understanding. I cannot explain it."

The angel said, "Stand up, and I will help you understand."

I said, "Please, my lord, speak to me, but do not leave me again, or I fear I will die too soon.

I have seen things I do not understand, and I have heard things that confuse me. Is my mind deceiving me? Am I only seeing a dream?

I beg you, my lord, explain this terrifying vision to me."

The angel answered, "Listen carefully, and I will teach you. I will reveal what you are afraid of, because the Most High has shared many secrets with you.

He has seen your righteous heart, how deeply you grieve for your people, and how much you mourn for Zion.

Now, here is the meaning of what you saw.

The woman who appeared to you in mourning—the one you tried to comfort—

She was not just a woman. She was Zion, the city you now see being built before you.

When she spoke of her son's misfortune, this is what it means:

The woman you saw is Zion itself, which has now become a great city.

When she told you she had been barren for thirty years, it represents the three thousand years before offerings were ever made there.

Then, after three thousand years, Solomon built the city and offered sacrifices in it. That is when the 'barren woman' finally bore a son.

When she spoke of raising her son with hardship, that represents the building and growth of Jerusalem.

When she said her son entered his wedding chamber and died, this symbolizes the fall and destruction of Jerusalem.

You saw how she mourned for her children, and you tried to comfort her.

Now, the Most High has seen how deeply you grieve for Zion, how your heart is truly broken for her suffering.

Because of this, He has allowed you to see her future glory and her true beauty.

That is why I told you to wait for me in the field, where no houses were built.

I knew the Most High was about to reveal these things to you.

That is also why I brought you to a place with no buildings—because no human structure could remain where the City of the Most High was about to be revealed.

But do not be afraid. Let your heart be at peace.

Go forward and see the light of Zion's glory. Look at the greatness of her buildings, as far as your eyes can see.

Then, you will hear as much as your ears can take in.

You are blessed above many others, for the Most High has chosen you among only a few."

Transition To the Fifth Vision {X. 58-59)

But tomorrow night, you must stay here.

The Most High will show you a vision of the events that will take place on earth in the last days.

Translated by Tim Zengerink

Vision V

(X. 60-XII. The Vision (X. 60---XII. Ja)

I stayed there that night, just as I was told.

The next night, I had a vision. I saw a huge eagle rising from the sea. It had twelve wings and three heads. As I watched, it spread its wings over the whole earth, and the winds from the sky blew around it. Clouds gathered toward it.

Then, I saw that smaller wings grew out of its large wings, but they were weak and unimportant. The eagle's heads remained still, but the middle head was larger than the others, even though it too was resting.

Then, the eagle commanded its wings to rule over the earth and its people. I saw that everything beneath the sky became subject to it, and no creature on earth resisted.

The eagle then stood on its claws and spoke to its wings, saying, "Go and rule over the earth. But rest now—do not all rise at once. Wake up at different times, and leave the heads for last."

I noticed that the eagle's voice did not come from its heads but from the middle of its body. I counted its small wings—there were eight.

Then, I saw one wing rise from the right side and rule over the earth. But after a while, it disappeared completely, leaving no trace.

Then, a second wing rose and ruled for a long time, but eventually, it too was destroyed like the first.

I heard a voice speaking to the second wing:

"You who have ruled for so long, listen! No ruler after you will hold power for as long as you did—not even for half as long."

Then, a third wing rose and ruled, just like the others, but it was also destroyed. The same happened to each of the wings—one after another, they ruled and then fell.

Later, I saw some of the smaller wings on the right side try to rule the earth. Some succeeded but were quickly destroyed. Others rose but never gained power.

Eventually, all twelve wings were gone, along with two of the small wings. All that remained of the eagle was its three resting heads and six small wings.

Then, I saw two of the small wings separate from the others and move under the right head, while the remaining four stayed in place.

I watched as these four small wings tried to rise to power. One of them succeeded but was quickly destroyed. The second tried, but it fell even faster than the first.

The last two small wings also thought they would rule, but before they could, something happened.

The middle head, which had been resting, suddenly woke up. It was larger than the other two heads.

It joined with the other two heads and turned on the last two small wings, devouring them before they could take power.

Then, the middle head ruled over the entire earth. It treated the people harshly and had more power than all the wings before it.

But suddenly, the middle head was destroyed, just like the wings had been.

Now, only the two remaining heads ruled over the earth and its people. Then, I saw the head on the right devour the head on the left, leaving only one.

Then, I heard a voice say, "Look ahead, Ezra, and see what happens at the end."

I looked and saw a lion coming out of the forest. It roared loudly, and then I heard it speak with a human voice. It spoke to the eagle, saying:

"Listen, eagle! I will tell you what the Most High says.

Are you not the one who remains from the…"

The Most High said, "I created four great beasts to rule over the world, and through them, the end of time would come.

You, the fourth beast, have risen above all the others before you. You have ruled over the earth with cruelty and have brought suffering to the whole world. You have lived among people for a long time, deceiving them and ruling unfairly.

You have stolen from the poor and mistreated those who are honest. You have harmed the humble, hated those who do what is right, and loved those who are deceitful. You have destroyed the homes of the successful and torn down the walls of those who never wronged you.

Because of your arrogance, your sins have reached the Most High.

Now, He has looked upon the times, and they have come to an end. The days He set in place have been fulfilled.

So, you, the eagle, will be completely destroyed—your great wings, your small and wicked wings, your cruel heads, your sharp claws, and your entire hateful body.

The earth will finally be at peace, free from violence. It will no longer suffer but will look forward to the judgment and mercy of its Creator."

Then, after the lion spoke these words to the eagle, I saw the last remaining head suddenly destroyed.

Then, the two wings that had tried to take power rose up to rule, but their rule was short and filled with chaos.

I watched as they too were destroyed, and the entire body of the eagle was burned. The earth stood in shock at what had happened.

The Interpretation of The Vision (XII. 3B-39)

I woke up in great distress and fear and said to myself, "This is happening to me because I have been seeking to understand the ways of the Most High.

Now, I feel completely drained, my spirit is weak, and I have no strength left because of the overwhelming fear I experienced last night.

But I will pray to the Most High, and He will give me the strength to endure."

Then I prayed, "Lord, if I have found favor in your eyes, if you have truly blessed me above many others, and if my prayers have reached you,

Then strengthen me and help me understand this vision I have seen. Please explain it to me so that my soul may find peace.

Did you not choose me to reveal the end of times and the completion of these events?"

Then He answered me, saying, "This is the meaning of the vision you saw:

The eagle that rose from the sea represents the fourth kingdom, the same one your brother Daniel saw in his vision. However, it was not explained to him as I am explaining it to you now.

A time will come when a kingdom will rise on the earth, more powerful and terrifying than all the kingdoms before it.

Twelve kings will rule over it, one after another. But the second king will rule longer than the others.

This is the meaning of the twelve wings you saw.

As for the voice that spoke, not from the eagle's head but from the middle of its body, this means that during the middle of that kingdom's reign, it will face many divisions and nearly collapse. However, it will not fall at that time but will recover and continue to rule.

The eight small wings that grew under its larger wings represent eight kings who will rise within the kingdom. Their reigns will be short and their rule unstable. Two of them will die early, four will be saved for the final period, and two will remain until the very end.

The three resting heads you saw represent three powerful kings that the Most High will bring at the end of this kingdom's time. They will change many things and will oppress the world and its people with even more cruelty than those before them.

That is why they are called the heads of the eagle—because they will bring its final wickedness before its end.

The one large head that was destroyed means that one of these kings will die naturally, though he will still suffer.

As for the two remaining kings, they will be killed by the sword. One will destroy the other, but in the end, he too will fall by the sword.

The two wings that moved to the head on the right side represent those whom the Most High has set apart for the final moments. Their rule will be short and filled with chaos, just as you saw.

The lion that came from the forest, roaring and speaking to the eagle, correcting it for its wickedness—this represents the Messiah.

The Most High has kept Him for the final days. He will come from the line of David and will confront the rulers of this world. He will call them out for their evil, expose their corruption, and show them their sins.

He will bring them before God for judgment while they are still alive. After He rebukes them, He will destroy them.

But He will show mercy to my people, those who have remained faithful and stayed within my borders. He will bring them joy until the final Day of Judgment arrives, just as I have told you before.

This is the vision you saw, and this is its meaning.

You alone have been chosen to understand this mystery of the Most High.

So write down everything you have seen in a book and keep it in a safe place.

Teach it only to those among your people who are wise and have the understanding to keep these secrets.

But you must remain here for seven more days, for the Most High will reveal even more to you."

Conclusion of The Vision (XII. 39B-48)

Then he left me.

When the people saw that seven days had passed and I had not returned to the city, they all gathered together—young and old—and came to me. They asked,

"What have we done wrong? How have we sinned against you that you have abandoned us and chosen to stay out here?

You are the last prophet left to us, like the last bunch of grapes from the harvest, like a light in the darkness, like a safe harbor for a ship caught in a storm.

Are all the troubles we have suffered not enough? Must we also lose you?

If you leave us too, then it would have been better if we had died when Zion was burned.

We are no better than those who perished there."

Hearing this, I cried out loudly and wept. Then I answered them,

"Have courage, Israel! Do not be discouraged, House of Jacob.

The Most High remembers you, and the Mighty One will not forget you forever.

I have not abandoned you, and I never will.

I came here to pray for the destruction of Zion and to ask for mercy for our Sanctuary, which has been humiliated."

Vision VI

(THE MAN FROM THE SEA)

(XIII. 1-58)

The Vision (XIII. 1-13a)

After seven days, I had a vision in the night. I saw a powerful wind rise from the sea, stirring up massive waves.

Then, from deep within the sea, a figure like a man appeared. He flew through the sky on the clouds of heaven. Everywhere he looked, the earth trembled before him. When he spoke, those who heard his voice melted away like wax in a fire.

Then, I saw an enormous army gathering from all directions, coming together to fight against the man who had risen from the sea.

I watched as he carved out a massive mountain for himself and stood on top of it. I wanted to see where the mountain had come from, but I couldn't find its source.

Even though the armies were terrified, they still prepared to fight him.

But he didn't raise his hand, pick up a spear, or use any weapon of war. Instead, he opened his mouth, and streams of fire, powerful winds, and burning coals poured out.

The fire, wind, and stormy flames combined and struck the army with overwhelming force. The entire multitude was instantly burned up, leaving nothing behind but ashes and smoke. I was shocked at what I saw.

Then, the man came down from the mountain and called out to another group of people, who peacefully came to him.

Many people approached him—some happy, some sad. Some were in chains, while others brought those who were to be offered.

At this point, I woke up in great distress. I prayed to the Most High and said,

"Lord, from the beginning, you have shown me these great wonders. Even though I am unworthy, you have answered my prayers.

Now, please reveal the meaning of this vision to me.

I fear for those who will be left alive in those days, but even more for those who will not survive.

Those who do not live to see these events will mourn what they have missed.

But those who do survive will suffer greatly, facing extreme dangers and hardships, as these visions have shown.

Yet, it is better to endure and witness these things than to disappear like a cloud and never see how the end of time unfolds."

Then He answered me, saying,

"I will explain your vision and also tell you about the people you have asked about.

As for those who survive and those who do not—here is the meaning:

Whoever endures the dangers of that time will be saved, as will those who have remained faithful and lived righteously before the Most High.

So know this—those who survive will receive more blessings than those who have died."

L. The Apocalypse of Ezra

The Interpretation of The Vision (XIII. 25-53A)

Here is what your vision means:

The man you saw rising from the sea is the one the Most High has been keeping for a long time. He will come to save creation and bring to safety those who remain.

The fire, storm, and breath that came from his mouth—without the use of weapons—destroying the army that gathered to fight him, means this:

The time is coming when the Most High will rescue those on earth. A great terror will fall upon the people.

Nations will turn against each other—cities against cities, places against places, people against people, and kingdoms against kingdoms.

When these signs take place, just as I told you before, my Son will be revealed—the same man you saw rising from the sea.

When people hear his voice, they will abandon their battles and conflicts.

Then, as you saw, an uncountable number of people will gather to fight against him.

But he will stand on Mount Zion, and Zion itself will appear before everyone—fully prepared and built, just as you saw the mountain that was not made by human hands.

My Son will confront these people for their wickedness, like a storm striking against them.

He will reveal all their evil deeds and the punishment they are about to face.

Then, like a blazing fire, he will destroy them effortlessly—by the Law of the One who is like fire.

The peaceful people he gathered afterward are the nine and a half tribes who were taken from their land during the time of King Josiah.

The Assyrian King Salmanassar captured them and took them to the other side of the Euphrates River, exiling them to a distant land.

But they made a decision among themselves—to leave behind the other nations and go to a place where no people had ever lived before.

There, they hoped to keep the Law that they had failed to follow in their own land.

They traveled through the narrow paths of the Euphrates, and the Most High performed miracles for them.

He held back the river's waters until they had all crossed safely.

Their journey was long—it took a year and a half—until they reached a place called Arsaph, at the farthest edge of the world.

They have lived there until the end times.

But when their return is near, the Most High will once again stop the flow of the Euphrates, so they can cross back.

That is why you saw a great gathering of people coming in peace.

The people from your own nation who remain within my sacred land will also survive.

When my Son destroys the gathered armies, he will protect those who are left, and then he will show them many wonders.

I then asked, "Lord, why did I see the man coming from the sea?"

He answered, "Just as no one can search the deep sea or fully know what lies beneath, no one on earth can see my Son or those with him—except in the time of his coming.

This is the meaning of your vision."

Transition To the Seventh Vision (XIII. 53B-58)

These things have been revealed to you alone

because you have set aside your own concerns and dedicated yourself to understanding the ways of the Most High. You have sought to learn the truths of the Law.

You have lived wisely and have treated understanding as your guide, like a mother who teaches her child.

That is why I have shown you these things—because the Most High has a reward for you.

In three days, I will speak to you again and reveal even greater wonders.

Then I went out into the field, walking for a long time, praising the Most High for the amazing things He has done throughout history.

I thanked Him for how He controls time and everything that happens within it.

And I stayed there for three days.

Vision VII

(Ch. XIV)

Ezra's Commission (XIV. 1-17)

After this, as I was sitting under an oak tree, a voice suddenly came from a bush in front of me.

It called out, "Ezra, Ezra!"

I answered, "Here I am!" and stood up.

The voice said, "I revealed myself from a bush and spoke with Moses when my people were enslaved in Egypt.

I sent him to lead my people out of Egypt, through the wilderness, and up to Mount Sinai. I kept him near me for many days,

showing him great wonders, revealing the secrets of time, and explaining how everything would come to an end.

I told him that some of these words must be kept secret, while others should be shared.

Now I say the same to you, Ezra.

The signs I have shown you, the visions you have seen, and the explanations you have heard—keep them in your heart and hide them.

Because you will be taken away from this world, and you will stay with my Son and others like you until the end of time.

This world is growing old, and its time is almost over.

So, put your life in order, warn your people, comfort those who are struggling, and guide the wise.

Let go of this temporary life,

free yourself from the concerns of this world, stop worrying about death, and cast away all weakness.

Do not let these thoughts trouble you—leave these times behind!

Because the troubles you have already seen will be followed by even greater ones.

As the world ages, evil will increase, and suffering will spread among its people.

Truth will fade, and lies will take over.

Look! The great eagle you saw in your vision is already on its way."

Ezra Prays for Inspiration (XIV. R8-26)

I answered and said, "Lord, please let me speak!

I will do as you have commanded and warn the people who are alive now. But what about those who have not yet been born? Who will warn them?

The world is covered in darkness, and its people have no light.

The Law has been burned, and no one knows the works you have done or what you are about to do.

If I have found favor in your eyes, Lord, send your Holy Spirit to me. I will write down everything that has happened in the world from the very beginning—everything written in your Law—so that people may find the right path and those who live in the last days will know the way.

He answered and said, "Go, gather your people, and tell them not to look for you for forty days.

Prepare many writing tablets, and take with you Seraia, Daria, Shelemia, Helkana, and Shiel—these five men, because they are skilled in writing quickly.

Come here, and I will place a light of understanding in your heart that will not go out until you have finished writing.

When you are done, you will share some of what you write with everyone, but some you must keep hidden and give only to the wise.

Tomorrow at this time, you will begin writing."

Ezra's Last Words (XIV. 27-36)

I went and did as I was commanded, gathering all the people together and saying to them:

"Listen, Israel, to these words.

Our ancestors were once strangers in the land of Egypt, but they were rescued from there.

They received the Law of life, but they did not follow it. And just like them, you have also broken it.

You were given the land of Zion as an inheritance, but you and your ancestors sinned and did not follow the ways that Moses, the servant of the Lord, commanded you.

So the Most High, who is a fair judge, took away what had been given to you for a time.

Now, you are suffering here, and your brothers and sisters have been scattered to a faraway land.

But if you turn back to the truth, discipline your hearts, and live rightly, you will be saved. And after death, you will receive mercy.

For after death, there will be judgment, and we will live again. Then, the names of the righteous will be honored, and the sins of the wicked will be exposed.

Until then, do not come near me or try to find me for forty days."

The Restoration of The Scriptures (XIV. 37-48)

I took the five men, just as I was commanded, and we went into the field, where we stayed.

The next day, a voice called out to me, saying, "Ezra, open your mouth and drink what I give you."

I opened my mouth and saw a full cup coming toward me. It looked like it was filled with water, but its appearance was like fire. I took the cup and drank from it.

As soon as I drank, my heart was filled with understanding, my mind overflowed with wisdom, and my spirit held onto knowledge. My mouth opened, and I could not stop speaking.

The Most High gave the five men the ability to understand, and they wrote down everything I spoke, using writing they had never known before.

I stayed there for forty days. During the day, I spoke, and they wrote. At night, they ate bread, but I remained awake, never stopping.

By the end of forty days, we had written ninety-four books.

When the forty days were over, the Most High spoke to me and said,

"The first twenty-four books you have written, make public. Let both those who are worthy and those who are not read them.

But keep the other seventy books hidden, and give them only to the wise among your people.

For in these books are the deep secrets of understanding, the sources of wisdom, and the path to knowledge."

I followed the command exactly, in the seventh year, during the sixth week, five thousand years after creation, on the twelfth day of the third month.

Conclusion Of the Book (XIV. 49-50)

After writing everything down, Ezra was taken away to be with others like him.

He was forever known as the Scribe of the Knowledge of the Most High.

This was the conclusion of Ezra's first account.

The Apocalypse of Peter

Many people will claim to be prophets, but they will spread false teachings that lead others down the wrong path. These false teachers will bring destruction upon themselves.

Then God will come to those who remain faithful—those who long for righteousness, endure hardships, and keep their souls pure in this life. He will bring justice against those who live in wickedness.

The Lord then said, "Let's go up to the mountain and pray."

So we, the twelve disciples, followed him. We asked him to show us one of our righteous brothers who had passed away, so we could understand what they were like. We hoped this would give us courage and help us inspire others to believe in our message.

As we prayed, two men suddenly appeared before the Lord, facing the east. Their faces shone as brightly as the sun, and their clothes sparkled with a brilliance beyond anything we had ever seen. Their beauty and glory were indescribable, and we could barely look at them.

We stared in amazement. Their bodies were whiter than the purest snow, yet at the same time, they had a soft red glow, like the petals of the most vibrant rose. The red and white blended perfectly, making them look even more magnificent.

Their curly hair shimmered and flowed over their shoulders like a crown made of fragrant flowers. It reminded me of a rainbow stretching across the sky. Their presence was breathtaking.

They had appeared so suddenly that we were left in complete awe.

I turned to the Lord and asked, "Who are these men?"

He answered, "These are your righteous brothers, the ones you wanted to see."

Then I asked, "Where do all the righteous live? What kind of place is it that gives them such beauty and glory?"

The Lord then revealed a vast and radiant land beyond this world. It was brighter than anything I had ever imagined, filled with pure light, as if the sun itself shone from within it. The air glowed with warmth, and the ground was covered in flowers that never faded, releasing a sweet and refreshing fragrance.

This land was full of beautiful, everlasting plants and trees that produced the most blessed fruit. Even from a distance, the scent of this paradise reached us, filling the air with its heavenly aroma.

The people in this place wore clothes as bright and beautiful as the robes of angels, matching the incredible beauty around them. Angels floated above, making the place even more breathtaking. Everyone there shared the same glory, and they sang together with one voice, praising God with joy.

The Lord said to us, "This is where your high priests and the righteous live."

But then, I saw another place—dark, filthy, and terrifying. It was a place of punishment. The air was thick and heavy, as gloomy as the dark clothing worn by both the punishing angels and those being punished. Some people were hanging by their tongues—these were the ones who had spoken against the righteous path. Beneath them, fire burned, causing them constant pain.

A huge lake of flaming mud was filled with people who had used righteousness for their own selfish gain. Tormenting angels caused them endless suffering. Nearby, women hung by their hair over the bubbling mud. They had dressed themselves to lure others into adultery. The men who had sinned with them hung by their feet, their heads sinking into the filthy, boiling mire.

I thought to myself, "I never imagined such a terrible place could exist."

I saw murderers and their accomplices thrown into a cramped space filled with venomous snakes. The snakes bit them over and over, making them twist and writhe in pain. Dark, crawling worms covered them like a thick cloud, adding to their suffering. The souls of the people they had killed stood nearby, watching and saying, "O God, your judgment is fair."

Not far from there, I saw another tight space where blood and filth from the suffering people drained into a pool, forming a lake. Women sat in the filthy liquid, submerged up to their necks. Across from them sat the children they had conceived but aborted. The children cried out, and sparks of fire shot from their mouths, burning the women's eyes. These were the women who had caused abortions and were now cursed for their actions.

Elsewhere, men and women burned up to their waists in a dark place while evil spirits beat them. Worms ate them from the inside, never stopping. These were the ones who had betrayed and attacked the righteous.

Nearby, some men and women chewed on their own lips in torment while burning irons were pressed into their eyes. They had spoken against righteousness and spread lies. Others bit their own tongues, and fire shot from their mouths—these were the false witnesses.

In another part of this place, sharp, burning-hot stones, sharper than swords, covered the ground. Men and women dressed in torn, dirty clothes rolled on them, suffering without end. These were the rich people who had put their trust in wealth, ignored orphans and widows, and disobeyed God's commands.

In a huge, bubbling lake filled with blood and filth, people stood knee-deep in the disgusting mixture. These were the greedy lenders who charged others unfair amounts of interest.

Others were thrown off a high cliff. When they hit the ground, they were forced to climb back up, only to be thrown down again, never finding rest. These were the men who had dishonored their bodies by acting like women and the women who had lain with each other like a man and woman should.

Next to the cliff, fire burned where men who had made idols for themselves stood, trapped in the flames. Nearby, other men and women carried rods, striking each other over and over without end.

In another place, men and women burned and twisted in agony. Their bodies roasted in the flames. These were the ones who had abandoned God's way to chase after their own selfish desires.

The Apocalypse of Paul

Introduction

The Acts of Paul and Thecla is an ancient Christian text from the second century that tells the story of Thecla, a noble young woman from Iconium, and how her life changed after meeting the Apostle Paul. Although it is part of a larger work called the Acts of Paul, this story became well-known on its own because of its exciting events and powerful themes.

In the story, Thecla is deeply moved by Paul's teachings about remaining pure and the promise of resurrection. She decides to leave her arranged marriage and go against her family's wishes to follow him. Because of her strong faith, she faces many dangers, including being sentenced to death by fire and thrown into an arena with wild animals. However, she miraculously survives each trial. In one striking moment, she even baptizes herself, showing her independence and deep belief in God.

This text also includes one of the earliest descriptions of Paul. He is described as a man of average height, with little hair, slightly bent legs, and large eyes. His eyebrows met in the middle, his nose was long, and he was known for his kindness and grace.

Scholars believe the Acts of Paul and Thecla was written sometime in the second century, possibly as early as 68–98 AD. A church leader named Tertullian later mentioned that a priest from Asia was removed from his position for writing it, showing that the text was seen as controversial in early Christian communities.

The story has had a lasting impact, especially in discussions about women's roles in the early church. Thecla's journey highlights themes of female strength, devotion, and the struggles faced by women who chose faith over traditional expectations. Her role as a preacher and baptizer has led to debates about whether women had leadership positions in early Christianity.

Even though the Acts of Paul and Thecla is not part of the official New Testament, it provides important insight into early Christian beliefs, the respect given to female figures, and the way gender and authority worked in ancient religious communities.

The Acts of Paul

As Paul traveled to Iconium after escaping from Antioch, he was accompanied by Demas and Hermogenes. These two men acted as if they were devoted followers, but they were not sincere. Paul, however, focused only on the goodness of Christ and did not treat them badly. Instead, he showed them kindness and spoke to them about Jesus, sharing details about His birth, resurrection, and the great things Christ had revealed to him.

A man named Onesiphorus heard that Paul was coming to Iconium. Wanting to welcome him, he went out with his wife Lectra and their children, Silas and Zeno. Titus had described what Paul looked like since Onesiphorus had never seen him in person, only in visions. He stood along the road to Lystra, watching travelers carefully, searching for Paul based on the description.

Then he saw Paul approaching. Paul was a small man, bald, with bowed legs, a strong build, thick eyebrows that met in the middle, and a long nose. But more than his appearance, he carried a presence full of grace—sometimes he looked like an ordinary man, and other times, his face shone like an angel's. When Paul saw Onesiphorus, he smiled.

Onesiphorus greeted him, saying, "Welcome, servant of the blessed God!"

Paul replied, "May grace be with you and your family."

Demas and Hermogenes, jealous of the special greeting, tried to act more devoted than they really were. Demas asked, "Are we not also servants of the blessed God? Why didn't you greet us the same way?"

Onesiphorus responded, "I do not see in you the actions of righteous men. But if you are truly faithful, you are welcome in my home as well."

Paul went into Onesiphorus' house, and everyone was filled with joy. They prayed together, broke bread, and Paul spoke about self-control and resurrection. He shared teachings such as:

"Blessed are those with pure hearts, for they will see God.

Blessed are those who keep their bodies pure, for they will be a home for God's spirit.

Blessed are those who practice self-control, for God will guide them.

Blessed are those who do not chase after worldly pleasures, for they will be called righteous.

Blessed are those who are married but remain devoted to God, for He will be their greatest reward.

Blessed are those who respect and honor the Lord, for they will be like angels.

Blessed are those who stay true to their baptism, for they will find peace with the Father and the Son.

Blessed are those who show kindness and mercy, for they will receive the same and will not suffer in judgment.

Blessed are those who remain pure, for they are pleasing to God and will not lose their reward.

The word of the Father will save them when His Son comes, and they will live in peace forever."

As Paul spoke in the church gathered at Onesiphorus' house, a young woman named Thecla sat by a nearby window, listening intently. She was the daughter of Theocleia and had been promised in marriage to a man named Thamyris. But as she heard Paul's teachings about purity and prayer, she was captivated, staying by the window day and night without looking away. She was deeply drawn to the faith and filled with joy as she listened.

When she saw many other women gathering to hear Paul, her desire grew stronger. She longed to be counted among them, to stand in Paul's presence, and to hear the message of Christ directly from him. Though she had never seen him before, his words alone had already touched her heart.

Thecla stayed by the window, listening intently, refusing to move. Seeing this, her mother, Theocleia, sent for Thamyris, her fiancé. Thamyris arrived happily, expecting to see Thecla, thinking their marriage would happen soon.

Theocleia turned to him and said, "Thamyris, I have something strange to tell you. For three days and nights, Thecla has not left the window. She refuses to eat or drink and keeps staring outside, as if she's watching something fascinating. She has become completely captivated by a foreign man who teaches strange ideas. I can't understand why my daughter, who has always been so modest, is behaving this way.

This man is dangerous—he is turning the whole city against our ways, including your Thecla. Both women and young men are going to listen to him, learning to fear God and live in purity. My daughter is trapped by his words like a spider in a web. She listens to everything he says with incredible focus, as if under a spell. Please, go talk to her—she is supposed to be your wife."

Thamyris approached Thecla, kissed her, and tried to hide his concern. "Thecla, my love, why are you sitting here like this? What has come over you? Look at me! Remember our engagement and be ashamed of this behavior."

Her mother also pleaded, "My child, why do you just sit there in silence, staring, acting as if you have lost your mind?"

They both cried—Thamyris, fearing he had lost his bride, and Theocleia, feeling as if she had lost her daughter. Even the servants grieved for their mistress, and the entire house was filled with sorrow. But Thecla didn't react. She didn't turn away from the window. She kept listening to Paul's words.

Frustrated, Thamyris stormed out into the street, watching people come and go from Paul's gathering. He spotted two men arguing and called out to them. "Tell me, who is this man leading people astray? He is deceiving young men and keeping women from getting married! If you can tell me who he is, I will pay you well—I am a wealthy and important man in this city."

Demas and Hermogenes, who had been pretending to follow Paul, saw an opportunity. "We don't know exactly who he is," they said, "but he tells people not to marry. He teaches that there is no true resurrection except for those who remain pure and do not corrupt their bodies."

Thamyris invited them to his house for a feast, serving them fine food and plenty of wine. He wanted to win them over so they would help him get Thecla back. As they ate, he asked, "Tell me about this man's teachings. I need to understand. I am deeply troubled because Thecla is obsessed with him, and I cannot marry her because of it."

Demas and Hermogenes gave him a plan. "Take him to the governor, Castelios. Accuse him of convincing people to follow new Christian beliefs, and the governor will deal with him quickly. Then you will be able to marry Thecla. We can also explain the so-called 'resurrection' he speaks of—it has already happened in our children. We were 'reborn' when we came to know the true God."

Hearing this, Thamyris was furious. The next morning, he gathered city leaders, public officials, and an angry crowd. Carrying clubs, they marched to Onesiphorus' house and shouted, "You have corrupted the people of Iconium! You have turned Thecla against me, and now she refuses to marry. Let's take him to the governor!"

The crowd chanted, "Away with this magician! He has tricked our wives and convinced many to change their beliefs!"

Thamyris stood before the governor and shouted, "This man is dangerous! He convinces young women to avoid marriage. Let him explain to you why he teaches these things!"

Demas and Hermogenes whispered to Thamyris, "Say that he is a Christian. That will be enough to get rid of him."

The governor, however, decided to question Paul directly. "Who are you?" he asked. "And what exactly do you teach? These men are accusing you of serious things."

Paul raised his voice and answered, "If you want to know what I teach, listen carefully. I serve the one true God, who is just and powerful. He does not need anything, but He cares about saving people. He sent me to lead them away from sin, corruption, and death, so they can live in holiness. That is why God sent His Son—whom I preach—to bring hope to the lost. He came to rescue the world from judgment, so that instead of punishment, people could have faith, fear God, live in holiness, and love the truth.

If this is what I teach, how am I doing anything wrong?"

The governor listened but was unsure of what to do. Instead of making a decision right away, he ordered Paul to be arrested and put in prison. "I will question him more when I have time," he said.

Late at night, Thecla took off her bracelets and gave them to the gatekeeper in exchange for letting her through. Once inside, she gave the jailer a silver mirror so she could visit Paul. She sat at his feet, listening to him speak about the greatness of God. Paul remained fearless, trusting completely in God, and Thecla's faith grew stronger. Moved by what she heard, she kissed the chains he was wearing.

Meanwhile, Thecla's family was searching for her. Thamyris, her fiancé, ran through the streets in a panic, asking where she had gone. One of the gatekeeper's fellow servants told them she had left during the night. When they questioned the gatekeeper himself, he admitted, "She went to see the foreigner in the prison."

They rushed to the prison and found Thecla sitting beside Paul, completely focused on his words. It was as if she were bound to him, not by chains, but by devotion. Furious, they gathered a crowd and reported everything to the governor. He immediately ordered Paul to be brought before him.

Thecla, however, remained where she was, lying on the ground where Paul had taught her. The governor then ordered her to be brought forward as well. But instead of fear, Thecla was filled with joy.

When Paul was brought before the crowd, people shouted angrily, "He is a magician! Get rid of him!" But the governor was curious and wanted to hear what Paul had to say about Christ. Afterward, he turned to Thecla and asked, "Why have you not obeyed Thamyris and followed the laws of Iconium?"

Instead of responding, Thecla kept her eyes on Paul. Seeing her silence, her mother became enraged and shouted, "Burn this disgraceful girl! If she refuses to marry, let her be burned in the theater! Let all women see what happens to those who listen to this man!"

The governor was deeply troubled. He ordered Paul to be beaten and thrown out of the city, and he sentenced Thecla to be burned. The crowd rushed to the theater, eager to see the punishment. Thecla, however, only looked around for Paul, like a lamb searching for its shepherd. As she scanned the crowd, she saw someone who looked like Paul sitting there. She said to herself, Even though I must face this, Paul has come to see me. She kept her eyes on him until, suddenly, he disappeared into the sky.

The servants and young women gathered wood to build the fire for her execution. As Thecla was led in, stripped of her clothes, the governor was moved to tears. Even as she stood there, about to be burned, he was amazed by the strength she carried within her.

The executioners prepared the fire, and Thecla made the sign of the cross before stepping onto the wood. The flames were lit, and a huge fire blazed around her. But miraculously, it never touched her. God showed her mercy—there was a sudden earthquake, and dark clouds covered the sky. A powerful storm brought down heavy rain and hail, pouring over the fire and putting it out. Many in the crowd were injured by the storm, but Thecla was unharmed.

Meanwhile, Paul had left Iconium with Onesiphorus, his wife, and children. They were fasting as they traveled toward Daphne. After several days without food, the children complained, "Paul, we are hungry, but we have no money to buy bread."

Onesiphorus had given up all his possessions to follow Paul, so they had nothing left. Paul took off his cloak and said, "Go, child, sell this and buy some bread."

As the boy went to buy food, he saw Thecla nearby and was stunned. "Thecla! Where are you going?"

She answered, "I survived the fire and am looking for Paul."

The boy excitedly told her, "Come with me! He has been praying for you for six days, worrying about what happened."

When Thecla arrived at the place where Paul was, he was kneeling in prayer, saying, "Lord Jesus, keep Thecla safe from the fire and protect her, for she belongs to You."

Hearing his words, Thecla cried out, "Father of heaven and earth, I bless You! You saved me so that I could find Paul again."

Paul stood up, saw her, and lifted his hands in praise. "God, who knows our hearts, Father of Jesus Christ, I bless You! You have answered my prayers so quickly."

They shared five loaves of bread, some herbs, and water, rejoicing in the works of Christ. Then Thecla turned to Paul and said, "I will cut my hair and follow you wherever you go."

But Paul cautioned her, "The world is cruel, and you are a beautiful young woman. I worry that you might face even greater challenges than before and might not be able to withstand them."

Thecla insisted, "Just baptize me in Christ, and no temptation will overcome me."

Paul responded, "Thecla, be patient. In time, you will receive baptism."

Paul then sent Onesiphorus and his family back to Iconium, while he and Thecla traveled to Antioch. As they entered the city, a powerful leader named Alexander saw Thecla and became infatuated with her. He tried to bribe Paul with gifts, hoping to win her over.

Paul, wanting to protect her, simply said, "I don't know the woman you're speaking of. She is not mine."

But Alexander was determined. He grabbed Thecla in the street, trying to claim her for himself. Thecla fought back, pushing him away. She called out, "Do not touch a servant of God! I am a noblewoman from Iconium, and because I refused to marry Thamyris, I was cast out of my city!"

She tore Alexander's cloak and knocked off the crown he wore on his head, humiliating him in public.

Embarrassed and angry, Alexander dragged her before the governor and accused her of attacking him. The governor asked if this was true, and Thecla admitted, "Yes, I did those things."

Hearing this, the governor sentenced her to be thrown to wild animals. Women in the crowd were shocked and shouted, "This is unfair! This is a cruel judgment!"

A noblewoman named Tryphaena, whose daughter Falconilla had died, felt sympathy for Thecla and took her in, treating her with kindness.

When the time came for her to face the wild animals, the soldiers tied Thecla to a fierce lioness, but instead of attacking her, the lioness lay down at her feet and licked them. The crowd watching was amazed.

The next day, they sent in more wild beasts, and Thecla stood, stretching her hands toward heaven in prayer. When she finished, she saw a pool of water nearby and said, Now is the time for me to baptize myself.

Ignoring the crowd's warnings, she jumped into the water, declaring, "In the name of Jesus Christ, I baptize myself!"

At that moment, lightning flashed, and the seals in the water died. A cloud of fire surrounded Thecla, covering her body so that no one could see her nakedness. The wild beasts could not come near her, and once again, she was saved.

As more wild animals were released into the arena, the women in the crowd wept. Some threw fragrant herbs like nard and cassia, filling the air with sweet scents. Yet, none of the animals touched Thecla. It was as if they had fallen into a deep sleep.

Frustrated, Alexander turned to the governor and said, "I have fierce bulls that will surely kill her. Let's tie her to them."

The governor, looking troubled, replied, "Do as you wish."

They tied Thecla's feet between two bulls and placed burning hot irons beneath them to make the animals panic and attack. The bulls ran wildly, but instead of harming her, the flames burned through the ropes, freeing Thecla completely.

Meanwhile, Tryphaena, who had been watching, fainted from shock. The people cried out, "Queen Tryphaena is dead!" Chaos spread through the city, and the governor ordered the games to stop.

Alexander, now afraid of the consequences, begged the governor, "Please have mercy on me and the city. Let this woman go. If Caesar hears about what happened, he will punish us, especially since Queen

Tryphaena has just collapsed beside the arena!"

The governor then called Thecla and asked, "Who are you? Why have none of the animals harmed you?"

Thecla answered, "I am a servant of the living God. I believe in His Son, in whom He is pleased. That is why no animal has touched me. He alone brings salvation and eternal life. He is a refuge for those in trouble, a comfort to the suffering, and hope for the lost. Those who do not believe in Him will not have eternal life."

The governor, amazed by her words, ordered her to be given clothes and allowed her to dress.

As she put on the garments, Thecla said, "The one who protected me while I was naked among the wild beasts will also clothe you with salvation on the day of judgment."

The governor then made an official announcement: "I release Thecla, a servant of God, who fears the Lord."

The women in the crowd cheered, shouting, "There is only one God—the God of Thecla!" Their voices were so powerful that the very foundations of the theater shook.

When Tryphaena heard the news, she rushed to meet Thecla and said, "Now I believe in the resurrection! Now I believe my daughter is alive! Come with me, and I will give you everything I have."

Thecla went with her and stayed in her home for eight days, teaching her about God. Even many of the servants in the household came to believe, and there was great joy.

After that, Thecla began searching for Paul and learned that he was in Myra, a city in Lycia. She dressed herself in a simple cloak, gathered a group of young men and women, and traveled there.

When she arrived, she found Paul preaching. Seeing her, Paul was surprised and worried, thinking she had been put on trial again. But Thecla ran to him and said, "Paul, I have received my baptism! The same God who worked through you for the Gospel has also worked in me for my baptism."

Paul took her to the home of a man named Hermæus, where she told him everything that had happened. Those who heard her story were amazed and encouraged. They all gathered in prayer for Tryphaena.

Then Thecla said, "I am going back to Iconium."

Paul blessed her, saying, "Go, and continue spreading the word of God."

Before she left, Tryphaena gave her many gifts, including fine clothes and gold. Thecla, in turn, gave much of it to Paul for helping the poor.

When she arrived in Iconium, she went straight to the house of Onesiphorus, where she had first heard Paul teach. She fell to the ground where Paul used to sit, crying as she prayed:

"God of this house, where You first shined Your light on me… Jesus Christ, Son of the living God, You were with me in the fire, You saved me from the wild beasts. May You always be glorified forever. Amen."

She discovered that Thamyris, her former fiancé, had died, but her mother was still alive. She sent for her mother and said, "Mother, do you now believe that the Lord rules in heaven? If you desire wealth, He has given it to you through me. If you desire your child, here I am beside you."

After speaking to her, Thecla left for Seleucia, where she lived in a cave for seventy-two years. She survived on herbs and water, sharing the word of God with many people.

However, some men in the city, who followed Greek beliefs and worked as doctors, became jealous of her. They saw how she healed the sick through faith, and since people no longer came to them for help, they wanted to get rid of her. They decided to send wicked men to attack her, believing that if she was harmed, she would lose her ability to heal.

But God protected her. As the men approached her cave, a rock suddenly opened, allowing Thecla to escape inside. The cave then closed behind her, leaving the men outside, unable to reach her. They only managed to tear a small piece of her veil.

Thecla then traveled to Rome, hoping to see Paul, but when she arrived, she found that he had already passed away. She stayed there for a short time before peacefully passing away herself.

Thecla was first thrown into the fire when she was seventeen and faced the wild beasts at eighteen. She lived in the cave for seventy-two years, dedicating her life to God. In total, she lived for ninety years. After healing many and spreading the Gospel, she passed away on September 24, resting among the saints in Christ Jesus. To Him be all glory and power forever. Amen.

Thank You for Reading

Dear Reader,

We hope this timeless classic has sparked your imagination and enriched your literary journey. Now that you've turned the final page, we want to share a vision for the future of reading—one where every classic you've ever wanted to explore is at your fingertips, in a format that best suits your life.

We'd like to invite you to gain immediate, unlimited digital & audiobook access to hundreds of the most treasured literary classics ever written—along with the option to secure deluxe paperback, hardcover & box set editions at printing cost. Together, we can spark a new global literary renaissance alongside our small, independent publishing house called "The Library of Alexandria."

Thousands of years ago, the Library of Alexandria stood as a beacon of knowledge—until it was lost to history. We aim to reignite that spirit of preservation and discovery right now, in the modern age—only this time, it's accessible to all, in every language and every format.

Picture a world where every timeless classic, novel, poem, or philosophical treatise is not only available to read but also updated for today's readers—modernized, translated into any language or dialect, and ready to enjoy in any format you choose, whether that is in an eBook, audiobook, paperback, or deluxe hardcover & box set version a printing cost.

By joining our movement to rebuild the modern Library of Alexandria, you become part of an unprecedented mission to offer:

- **Unlimited Audiobook & eBook Access to the Greatest Classics of All Time**

  Instantly explore thousands of legendary works, from Plato and Shakespeare to Jane Austen and Leo Tolstoy. All are instantly ready to read or listen to, giving you a complete literary universe at your fingertips.

- **Paperback & Deluxe Editions at Printing Costs:**

  Purchase any title in a paperback, deluxe hardbound, or deluxe boxset edition at printing costs, shipped right to your doorstep. Curate your personal library of Alexandria with editions worthy of display—crafted to last, designed to captivate, and delivered straight to your door.

- **Modern translations for Contemporary Readers in all languages and dialects**

  Discover a vast selection of classics reimagined in clear, current language—no more struggling with outdated phrases or obscure references. Next to the original versions, we aim to offer translations in as many languages and dialects as possible.

  As we continue our translation efforts and add new languages, readers everywhere can connect with these works as if they were written today. By bridging linguistic divides, you're contributing to ensuring that these timeless stories become more meaningful, accessible, and inspiring for people across the globe.

- **Your Personal Library of Alexandria:**

  Over the months and years, you'll curate a unique physical archive of classics—each volume a testament to your taste, curiosity, and love of knowledge. It's not just about owning books—it's about curating a cultural legacy you'll cherish and pass down for generations to come.

- **Join a Global Literary Renaissance:**

    Your support fuels an ongoing mission: allowing us to reinvest in offering deluxe print editions (including special boxsets) at their true cost, broaden the range of available formats and translations, and extend the reach of these works to new audiences worldwide. By joining today, you're not just preserving a legacy of masterpieces; you set in motion a powerful wave of literary accessibility.

    We are more than a publisher—we're a movement, and we can't do it alone. Your support lets us scale our mission, preserving and reimagining history's greatest works for tomorrow's readers.

Become a Torchbearer of knowledge.

Thank you for picking up this book and allowing us into your literary journey. As you turn the pages, know that you're part of something larger: a global effort to keep these stories alive, share their wisdom across borders and generations, and spark a true cultural revival for the modern era.

If this resonates with you—please consider taking the next step by visiting:

www.libraryofalexandria.com

With gratitude and a shared love of knowledge,

The Modern Library of Alexandria Team

Visit:

www.libraryofalexandria.com

Or scan the code below: